Elisabeth Pfeiffer

Pop & Rock Ukulele

Fingerstyle Etüden

Fingerstyle Etudes

Title: Pop & Rock Ukulele: Fingerstyle Etüden - Fingerstyle Etudes
Author: Elisabeth Pfeiffer
Lektorat/Copy-Editing: Sanne Glaesemer-Seiler, Konrad Naegeli, Tara Maysay

Layout, Score and Photo-Illustrations: Elisabeth Pfeiffer
Cover-Design: Sorin Radulescu
Font: Raleway
Picture "Right Hand": Freepik licensed by CC BY 3.0, edited by Elisabeth Pfeiffer
Icon Video: made by Catalin Fertu from Flaticon is licensed under Creative Commons by CC BY 3.0

Publisher:
Elisabeth Pfeiffer
Ablestr.23
84508 Burgkirchen, Germany
info@poprockukulele.de

Audio Recordings and Mastering: Elisabeth Pfeiffer
Ukulele: by i'Iwi Ukuleles, Honolulu, Hawaii
Recorded April 2020
ISBN: 9798639500473
Imprint: Independently published
Printed by CreateSpace

Elisabeth Pfeiffer

Pop & Rock Ukulele
Fingerstyle Etüden
Fingerstyle Etudes

30 Etüden zu
Zupfmustern und Klang

*30 Fingerstyle Etudes to
Develop your Picking Technique and Sound*

Kostenlose Audiodateien
und Videos

Free Audio and Video

Ausführliche Anmerkungen
und Übetipps zu jedem Stück

*Extensive Performance and
Practice Notes on Each Piece*

ZUR AUTORIN

Elisabeth Pfeiffer studierte klassische Gitarre in Appleton, WI, USA und an der Hochschule für Musik, Würzburg, wo sie 2007 mit Diplom abschloss. Seit 2013 beschäftigt sie sich mit der Ukulele und mittlerweile sind drei Lehrbücher ihrer Buchreihe „Pop- und Rock-Ukulele" erschienen, in denen sie verschiedene Schlag- und Zupftechniken, sowie Griffbrettkonzepte vermittelt. Auf der Bühne spielt sie eigene Solo-Arrangements beliebter Lieder aus Pop, Rock und Jazz, Renaissancemusik und Neue Musik und erweitert das Repertoire der Ukulele, indem sie Kompositionsaufträge vergibt.

ABOUT THE AUTHOR

Elisabeth Pfeiffer majored in classical guitar, both at Lawrence University, Appleton, WI, USA and Hochschule für Musik, Würzburg, Germany, where she graduated in 2007. In 2013 she took up a ukulele and never looked back. Since, she has written three method books on strumming and picking techniques and fretting concepts. On stage she mostly performs solo pieces, but throws in the occasional song, always looking to add something personal to a piece or a song. She plays arrangements from Renaissance music to Jazz and is working on expanding the solo repertoire for the ukulele with her own arrangements and by commissioning compositions.

'Im Leben geht es vor allem darum, bewusst im Sinne seines Ansinnens zu handeln.'

Pablo Casals

'The first thing to do in life is to do with purpose what one purposes to do.'

Pablo Casals

CONTENT   INHALT

INTRODUCTION

Welcome to 'Fingerstyle Etudes', a collection of Ukulele etudes! This book comes to you in both English and German and aims to reach ukulele players, who have been playing for a while and are familiar with standard chords. every piece is based on a specific picking pattern; there is hardly any strumming in this book. You'll get pieces for every level. From the next page onwards you'll find instructions on how to work with this book.

The compositions in this book are quite atmospheric and work regardless whether you play them fast or slow. Most pieces come without tempo or dynamic indications. Please find your own interpretation and don't hesitate to show me your version on Facebook, Instagram or via email.

As you might know, every book of the **Pop & Rock Ukulele - Series** comes with audio and video files, that you can download. There is video of me playing every piece and the sound of the video is seperately available as an audio file to give you the chance to hear my interpretation.

You can get the link on

www.poprockukulele.de/downloads

or if you drop me a line at

info@poprockukulele.de .

I hope, you'll have tons of fun with the book! Please don't hesitate to contact me with questions or comments.

Good luck and best wishes,

Elisabeth Pfeiffer

EINLEITUNG

Willkommen zur Etüdensammlung ,Fingerstyle Etüden'! Dieses zweisprachige Buch richtet sich an Ukulelespieler, die schon eine Weile spielen und mit den Grundakkorden vertraut sind. Alle Stücke basieren auf bestimmten Zupfmustern; Schlagmuster kommen so gut wie gar nicht vor. Du wirst Stücke in allen Schwierigkeitsgraden finden. Genaue Anweisungen zum Umgang mit dem Buch findest du ab der nächsten Seite.

Die Kompositionen in diesem Buch sind recht atmosphärisch und funktionieren unabhängig davon, ob sie schnell oder langsam gespielt werden. Bei den meisten Stücken ist keine Tempoangabe oder Dynamik angegeben. Finde bitte deine eigene Interpretation und zögere nicht, mir deine Version per Facebook, Instagram oder Email zu zeigen.

Wie schon bei den anderen Büchern der **Pop- und Rockukulele - Reihe**, kannst du Audio- und Videodateien downloaden. Jedes Stück ist einmal als Video vorhanden und die Tonspur des Videos gibt es separat als Audiodatei, damit du meine Interpretation der Stücke hören kannst.

Den Link bekommst du unter

www.poprockukulele.de/downloads

oder unter

info@poprockukulele.de.

Ich wünsche dir viel Spaß mit diesem Buch! Melde dich bei Fragen oder Anregungen.

Viele liebe Grüße und viel Erfolg,

Elisabeth Pfeiffer

Anleitung

Instructions

HOW TO WORK WITH THIS BOOK

This book contains repertoire pieces in varying levels of difficulty. Every piece concentrates on a picking pattern which you can see underneath the title of a piece on the right. In this part of the page, you'll also find brief references to additional technical content of that piece. Etudes with the same picking pattern are grouped together, which means that a beginner's etude can be followed by an advanced one, because both feature the same picking pattern.

However, I've generally tried to place easier content towards the beginning of the book, while more advanced picking patterns move towards the back of the 'Repertoire'-part.

Every etude takes up two double pages of this book. The first two pages show the piece in music and tabs on the right page, as well as 'Practice and Performance Notes' and fretboard diagrams on the left page.

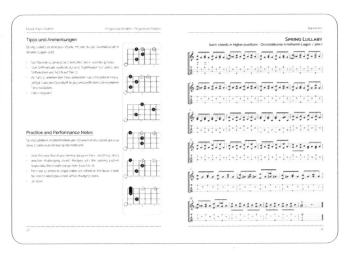

MIT DIESEM BUCH ARBEITEN

In diesem Buch findest du Spielstücke in ganz unterschiedlichen Schwierigkeitsgraden. Bei allen Stücken steht jeweils ein Zupfmuster im Mittelpunkt und wird oben rechts unter dem Titel angegeben. Dort findest du auch kurze Hinweise zu weiteren technischen Inhalten des Stückes. Spielstücke mit gleichen Zupfmustern stehen zusammen, sodass auf eine sehr einfache Etüde unmittelbar eine fortgeschrittene folgen kann, weil beide dasselbe Zupfmuster zum ,Thema' haben.

Grundsätzlich habe ich mich aber darum bemüht, den Schwierigkeitsgrad von vorne nach hinten ansteigen zu lassen. Grundlegende Zupfmuster stehen also eher am Anfang des Repertoire-Teiles, fortgeschrittene Zupfmuster eher am Ende.

Jede Etüde wird auf zwei Doppelseiten vorgestellt. Die erste Doppelseite enthält das Stück in Noten und Tabulatur auf der rechten und zugehörige ,Tipps und Anmerkungen' , sowie Griffbilder auf der linken Seite.

Die jeweils anschließende Doppelseite (siehe umseitig) enthält einerseits das Stück nur als Tabulatur-Ausgabe auf der linken und eine Version nur in Notenschrift auf der rechten Seite. Die Noten-Version enthält ausführliche Fingersätze für die Greifhand.

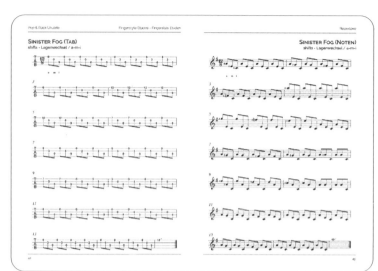

The following double page shows the piece in tab-only and music-only versions. The music version features elaborated fingerings for your fretting hand.

FINGERSÄTZE

FINGERINGS

Die Finger der Greifhand sind nummeriert: 1, 2, 3 und 4. Leere Saiten werden mit 0 bezeichnet.

Die Finger der Zupfhand sind nach den Spanischen Wörtern für die Finger benannt: pulgar - Daumen, indice - Zeigefinger, medio - Mittelfinger, anular - Ringfinger.

Kurz: p für Daumen
       i für Zeigefinger
       m für Mittelfinger
       a für Ringfinger

Fretting hand fingerings: your fingers are numbered 1, 2, 3 and 4. Open strings are numbered 0.

Picking hand fingers are named after the Spanish words for them: pulgar - thumb, indice - index finger , medio - middle finger, anular - ring finger.

Short: p for thumb
        i for index finger
        m for middle finger
        a for ring finger

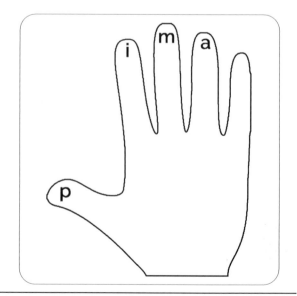

READING TABS

Tabs or Tabulature is probably the oldest way to notate music for stringed instruments. Tabs always tell you which string to pluck and where to fret it. Sometimes they also tell you the rhythm of the notes.

In this book, I've used two different types of tabulature:

When a new piece is first introduced, you find it in music and tabs. The tabs in this version don't show any rhythm, since you can easily see that in the music above the tab staff.

Between the music and the tab staff at the

TABULATUR LESEN

Tabulatur oder Tabs ist wahrscheinlich die historisch älteste Notationsmethode für Saiteninstrumente. Tabs sagen dir immer welche Saite du zupfen und wo du sie greifen sollst. Manchmal gibt die Tabulatur auch Auskunft über den Rhythmus der Noten.

In diesem Buch gibt es zwei verschiedene Arten von Tabulatur:

Wird ein Stück zum ersten Mal vorgestellt, ist es in Noten und Tabulatur aufgeschrieben. In diesem Fall habe ich den Rhythmus in den Tabs weggelassen, weil du ihn gut in den Noten über der Tabulaturzeile sehen kannst.

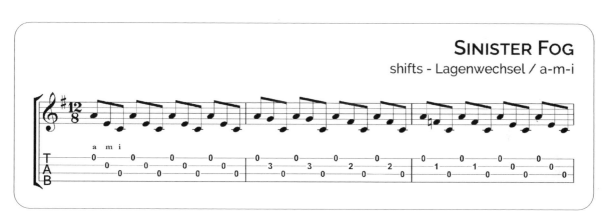

SINISTER FOG

shifts - Lagenwechsel / a-m-i

beginning of the piece, you'll always find the picking pattern corresponding with the single notes.

In our example above you start out plucking the open a-string (0) with the a-finger, then the open e-string (0) with your m-finger and the open c-string (0) with you i-finger. Repeat that four times, before fretting the e-string on the third fret (3) and then later on the second fret (2).

Apart from the music and tab version of a piece, every etude is additionally provided

Das Zupfmuster in Bezug auf die Einzeltöne steht immer am Anfang des Stückes zwischen der Noten- und der Tabulaturzeile.

Im Beispiel oben zupfst du zunächst die leere a-Saite (0) mit dem a-Finger, dann die leere e-Saite (0) mit dem m-Finger und schließlich die leere c-Saite (0) mit dem i-Finger. Dieser Ablauf wiederholt sich viermal, bevor du im nächsten Takt die e-Saite erst am dritten Bund (3) und später am zweiten Bund (2) greifst.

Neben der Noten und Tabulatur Version eines Stückes wird jede Etüde auch als reine Tabulatur Version angeboten. Die Tabs dieser Version funktionieren genauso, wie oben erklärt, stehen zusätzlich aber in Rhythmusno-

in a tab-only version. The tabs in this version work much the same way as explained above, but offer rhythmical notation as well. In this case, every tab number is an eighth note.

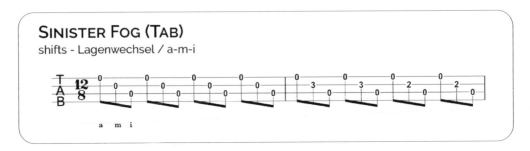

tation. Hier stehen jeweils Achtelnoten an den Tabulaturzahlen.

GRIFFBILDER LESEN

Die Griffbilder in diesem Buch entsprechen der Tabulaturansicht der Stücke. Ein Griffbild bildet jeweils maximal 6 Bünde auf der Ukulele ab. Die horizontalen Linien stehen von unten nach oben für die Saiten g, c, e und a der Ukulele. Die vertikalen Linien stellen die Bundstäbchen dar. Schwarze Punkte mit Zahlen sind ‚feste' Griffe, Ankerfinger die liegenbleiben können oder Ausgangsgriffe für

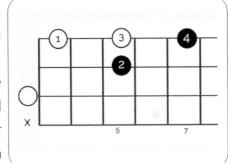

eine mehrtaktige Strecke des Stückes. Die Zahlen schlagen entsprechende Finger vor, mit denen zu greifen ist. Die weißen Punkte mit Zahlen zeigen Töne, die später verwendet werden. Leere weiße Punkte stellen leere Saiten dar, und sind deshalb immer am linken Rand des Griffbildes zu finden. Kreuze (x)

READING CHORD DIAGRAMS

The chord diagrams in this book correspond directly with the tabs for each piece. Each chord diagram shows a maximum of 6 frets on your uke. Horizontal lines represent the strings: from the bottom up G, C E and A. Vertical lines represent fretwires. Black dots with numbers are fixed chords, anchor fingers or starting positions for a series of fretting actions over the course of a few bars in the piece. Numbers are suggestions for fretting fingers you can use. White dots with numbers show notes that are temporarily added or changed. Empty white dots are open strings and therefore found on the left side of the chord diagram. X-signs mark strings that are not to be played. Fret numbers are below the chord diagram.

In the example you can see above you place

your fretting hand's middle finger (2) on the e-string on the 5th fret and keep it there throughout. Your pinky frets the 7th fret on the a-string and is lifted sometime during this section of the piece. Your index (1) and Ring-finger (3) fret different notes on the a-string. Repetitive open strings (like the c-string in this case) are always a logical consequence to the picking pattern that the piece is based on.

I've tried hard to translate as much of the music and tabs into chord diagrams as possible. However, it wasn't possible to show every situation of a piece. Chord diagrams give you an idea about how to approach a piece and show tricky spots. They'll also give you an idea of the level of a piece.

READING MUSIC

Sheet music is certainly the most comprehensive way to notate any musical piece. However, reading music can be complex and some knowledge is needed to make the most of it. Obviously, it's not possible to explain every detail about reading music on a few pages. Here are a few basics that should help you find your way throughout the book. And while working with this book, you'll have the unique opportunity to practice how to read music, by comparing the different versions of each piece.

Ukulele-tabs work with four lines represent-

bezeichnen Saiten, die nicht gespielt werden. Bundzahlen stehen unterhalb des Griffbildes. Im obigen Beispiel greift der Mittelfinger der Greifhand (2) am 5. Bund auf der e-Saite und bleibt dort liegen. Der kleine Finger (4) greift zunächst auf dem 7. Bund der a-Saite, wird aber dann im Verlauf des Stückes abgehoben und der Zeige- (1) und Ringfinger (3) überneh-men andere Töne auf der a-Saite. Die c-Sai-te ist jeweils mit dabei. Leere Saiten ergeben sich immer logisch aus dem Zupfmuster, das dem Stück zugrunde liegt. Ich habe versucht, möglichst umfangreich die Noten und Tabu-laturen der Stücke in Griffbilder zu überset-zen. Es war aber nicht immer möglich, jede Griffsituation darzustellen. Griffbilder geben dir einen Eindruck, wie du an das Stück ran-gehen kannst und zeigen knifflige Stellen. Du bekommst von den Griffbildern auch einen Eindruck davon, wie schwer das Stück ist.

NOTEN LESEN

Noten geben die umfangreichste Auskunft über die aufgeschriebene Musik, sind aller-dings auch etwas komplexer zu lesen und benötigen einiges Wissen. Es ist natürlich nicht möglich das Notenlesen wirklich um-fassend auf ein paar Seiten zu erklären. Hier findest du eine kleine Einführung, die es dir leichter machen soll, dich in diesem Buch zu-recht zu finden. Und in der Arbeit mit diesem Buch hast du die Gelegenheit, Notenlesen im direkten Vergleich der verschiedenen Versio-nen derselben Stücke zu üben.

Im Gegensatz zu den vier Linien der Ukule-

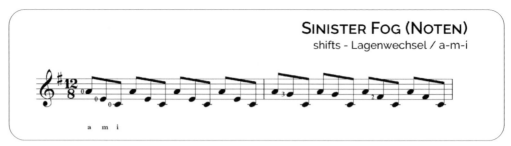

lentabulatur, die die Saiten der Ukulele darstellen, besteht eine Notenzeile aus fünf Linien. Je nach Verortung des Notenkopfes in diesem System aus Linien und Zwischenräumen, wird eine bestimmte Tonhöhe dargestellt. Ganz am Anfang der Notenzeile steht ein Notenschlüssel, in unserem Fall der sogenannte ‚Violinschlüssel' oder ‚g-Schlüssel'. Es gibt weitere Notenschlüssel, die für uns hier allerdings nicht wichtig sind. Der ‚g-Schlüssel' definiert in dem Fadenkreuz seines Bauches, den Ton g, der in diesem Fall auf der zweiten Linie der Notenzeile liegt.

Ein recht hilfreiches Werkzeug beim Finden

ing the strings of the uke. Music staffs have five single lines. Depending on the location of the note head in this system of lines and spaces, the music tells you which pitch to play. The clef at the start of the music staff in our case is a 'treble clef' or 'G-clef'. Other clefs exist, but they're not important for us right now. The 'G-clef' defines in his cross-hair the note g, located on the second line of the staff. A helpful tool to start finding pitches in the staff is the so-called 'natural note series' Western music is based on.

einzelner Noten in der Notenzeile ist die sogenannte ‚Stammtonreihe'. Der Ton h wird hier in amerikanischer Schreibweise als b bezeichnet.

Wenn wir nun zum oberen Beispiel zurückgehen, sehen wir, dass der erste Ton des Stückes ‚a' heißt. Die ‚a-Saite' ist nach der Tonhöhe (‚a') benannt, die erklingt, wenn wir die Saite spielen.

Going back to our example above, you can now find out the name of the first note, which is 'a'. The 'a-string' is named after the pitch ('a') that sounds, when we play the open string.

This is the fingerboard of your uke showing the locations of single notes of the natural note series for reference.

Auf dieser Darstellung des Griffbretts deiner Ukulele siehst du, wo die einzelnen Töne der Stammtonreihe zu finden sind.

Du musst nicht nicht das ganze Griffbrett aus-

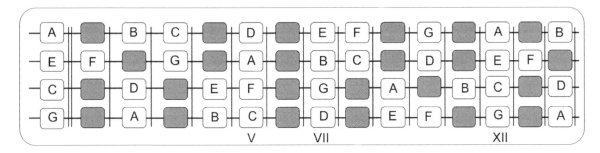

Please do not try and memorize all the notes, but refer to this when needed.

wendig lernen. Schau hier nach, wenn es notwendig ist.

Töne der Stammtonreihe können durch Vorzeichen oder Versetzungszeichen verändert werden.

The notes of the natural note series can be altered by accidentials.

Sharps make a note sound a 'half-step' higher. This means for us that we find the note one fret closer to the soundhole on the same string.

Flats make a note sound a half-step lower. It's now one fret closer to the headstock of your uke.

Naturals return an altered note to its original pitch of the natural note series.

Kreuzzeichen erhöhen den Ton um einen ‚Halbton'. Für uns bedeutet das, dass der Ton einen Bund Richtung Schallloch auf der gleichen Saite zu finden ist.

Das b-Vorzeichen erniedrigt den Ton um einen Halbton. Er befindet sich jetzt einen Bund weiter Richtung Ukulelenkopf.

Das Auflösungszeichen führt eine veränderte Note wieder zur ursprünglichen Tonhöhe der Stammtonreihe zurück.

Accidentials right in front of a single note are valid for one bar only. If an accidental shows up at the beginning of a staff, it's valid for the whole piece and is called key signature.

If you go back to the fretboard on the previous page, you'll see grey squares. Depending on the side you 'approach' them from, they can be filled with a sharpened or a flattened note.

Wenn das Versetzungszeichen unmittelbar vor einer Note steht, gilt es bis zum Ende des Taktes. Steht es am Anfang der Notenzeile gilt es das ganze Stück über und heißt dann Vorzeichen.

Wenn du zur Griffbrettdarstellung auf der letzten Seite zurück gehst, siehst du graue Felder. Je nachdem, von welcher Seite du rangehst, kannst du sie mit erhöhten oder erniedrigten Tönen auffüllen.

Neben der Tonhöhe ist die Tondauer für's Notenlesen wichtig. Diese Aufstellung zeigt die wichtigsten Notenwerte, die miteinander in Relation stehen.

Die Ganze Note dauert doppelt so lange, wie die Halbe Note. Die Halbe Note dauert doppelt so lange, wie die Viertelnote. Die Viertelnote dauert doppelt so lange, wie die Achtelnote

Ganze Note	𝅝	whole note
Halbe Note	𝅗𝅥	half note
Viertelnote	♩	quarter note
Achtelnote	♪	eighth note
Sechzehntelnote	𝅘𝅥𝅯	sixteenth note

und die Achtelnote dauert doppelt so lange, wie die Sechzehntelnote.

In diesem Buch ist vor allem wichtig, dass gleiche Notenwerte auch gleich lange dauern. Die meisten Stücke sind entweder in Achtel- oder Sechzehntelnoten notiert. Das bedeutet NICHT, dass die Etüden schneller oder langsamer gespielt werden! Du kannst Sechzehntelnoten sehr langsam und Achtelnoten sehr schnell spielen. Es ist nur wichtig, dass die Töne alle gleichmäßig und gleich lang gespielt werden.

Das Stück ist in Takte gegliedert. Einzelne Takte werden durch Taktstriche voneinander getrennt. In der Musik gibt es verschiedene Taktarten. Die meisten Stücke in diesem Buch stehen im 4/4 Takt. Das bedeutet, dass ein Takt vier Viertelnoten enthält (das sagt wieder nichts über das Tempo des Stücks aus!): Viertelnoten werden normalerweise in zwei Achtelnoten geteilt. Zähle also: 1 ‚und' 2 ‚und' 3

The length of a note, aside from the pitch, is important for reading music. This list gives you the most important note values that relate to one another.

A whole note is twice as long as a half note. A half note is twice as long as a quarter note. A quarter note is twice as long as an eighth note. An eighth note is twice as long as a sixteenth note.

For this book, it's important to realize that the same note values take up the same amount of time. Most pieces are notated either in eighth or sixteenth notes.

This does NOT mean that the etudes should be played faster or slower! You can play very slow sixteenth notes or very fast eighth notes. The only thing that is important is, that all of the notes are played evenly at the same speed (tempo).

The time of music is organized in different meters and bars. Single bars are seperated by barlines. Most of the pieces in this book stand in 4/4-time, which means, one bar contains 4 quarter notes (again, this does not say anything about the tempo: the quarter notes are usually divided into two eighth notes, so count 1 'and' 2 'and' 3 'and' 4 'and'. There are four sixteenth notes to a quarter note. Count 1-e-and-a-2-e-and-a-3-e-and-a-4-e-and-a.

The time signature can be found at the beginning of the piece. The lower number specifies the type of note to a bar, the upper number the number of said notes to one bar. There are pieces in 2/4-, 3/4-, 6/8- and 12/8-time. 3/4-meter is a classic waltz. Count 1-2-3 1-2-3. 6/8-meter is more fluid and the stressed notes are on 1 and 4. Count 1 2 3 4 5 6.

‚und' 4 ‚und'. Vier Sechzehntelnoten passen in eine Viertelnote. Zähle 1-e-un-de 2-e-un-de 3-e-un-de 4-e-un-de.

Die Taktart steht am Anfang des Stücks. Die untere Zahl spezifiziert die Art von Note für den Takt; die obere Zahl gibt die Anzahl von solchen Noten pro Takt an. Du wirst hier Stücke im 2/4-, 3/4-, 6/8- und 12/8-Takt finden. Der 3/4-Takt ist der klassische Walzer. Zähle 1-2-3 1-2-3. Der 6/8-Takt fließt mehr und die betonten Noten liegen auf der 1 und der 4. Zähle 1 2 3 4 5 6.

TECHNICAL CONCEPTS OF THIS BOOK

TECHNIKKONZEPTE IN DIESEM BUCH

Preparing picking fingers: Preparation is crucial for good sound and confident picking skills. The idea is to place the fingers on the string they're about to pick, BEFORE they'll pick it. Subsequently separating the picking movements into two independent parts.

In a picking pattern preparation works like this: for the picking pattern p-i-m-a place all four fingers on their respective strings and keep each finger on the string until it's its turn. After the finger has picked it'll stay up in the air until all fingers are up in the air after you've picked your a-finger. Then place all of your fingers on the four strings at the same time and repeat the picking pattern in the same fashion, keeping each finger on the string until it's its turn. This gives you a very controllable moment and a reset before every picking pattern. This way of preparing is called the 'full plant', because you plant every possible finger on

Vorbereiten (Zupfhand): Vorbereiten ist eine wichtige Voraussetzung für einen guten Klang und kontrolliertes Anschlagen der Saite. Die Finger der Zupfhand werden an die Saiten gelegt, BEVOR sie angeschlagen werden. Dabei wird das Berühren der Saite vom Anschlagen entkoppelt.

Vorbereiten funktioniert so: im Zupfmuster p-i-m-a werden alle vier Finger an die entsprechenden Saiten gelegt und dort liegen gelassen, bis sie an der Reihe sind. Wenn ein Finger seine Saite angeschlagen hat bleibt er in der Luft, bis alle Finger (nach dem Anschlag des a-Fingers) sich nicht mehr an den Saiten befinden. Dann werden alle vier Finger wieder gleichzeitig auf die Saiten gelegt und das Zupfmuster wird wieder so angeschlagen, dass jeder Finger an seiner Saite bleibt bis er dran ist. Das ermögicht einen sehr kontrollierbaren Moment und einen Neustart vor jedem Zupfmuster. Das oben beschriebene ,vollständige Vorbereiten' heißt so, weil alle Finger, die möglich sind gleichzeitig an die Saiten gelegt werden. In meinem Buch ,Pop- und Rock-Ukulele: Zupfmuster' beschreibe ich noch andere Möglichkeiten Vorzubereiten. Für dieses Buch brauchst du eigentlich nur folgende Regel:

Alle Finger aus der ,Basis-' Reihenfolge ,p-i-m-a' können gleichzeitig vorbereitet werden. Das heißt z.B. beim Zupfmuster p-a-m-i können p und a vorbereitet werden. Bei a-m-i kann nur a vorbereitet werden (aber p liegt bei den Stücken in diesem Buch dann auf der g-Saite) und bei p-i-a-m kannst du p, i und a, aber nicht m vorbereiten.

Dahinter steht der Gedanke, dass Finger, die die Saiten berühren, deine Hand stabilisieren und dir so einen gezielteren und sichereren Anschlag ermöglichen.

Saitenkontakt oder Saitengefühl ist eine direkte Folge von Vorbereiten. Es bezeichnet das bewusste Wahrnehmen der Finger an den Saiten.

Ankerfinger ist ein Finger der auf einem bestimmten Ton liegen bleibt, während sich der Griff drumherum verändert. Du kannst anfängliche durch folgende Übung beheben: Greife den Akkord und klopfe dann jeden Finger einzeln ein paarmal auf seinen Bund, während die anderen Finger liegen bleiben. Diese Klopfübung kann auf jeden Griff angewendet werden.

Stell' dir vor, wie Wurzeln aus deiner Fingerkuppe ins Griffbrett wachsen. Hebe dann die anderen Finger einzeln ab.

the strings at the same time. There are other ways of preparing described in my book 'Pop & Rock Ukulele: Picking'. For this book there's only one rule you could work on implementing: Fingers of the 'original sequence' p-i-m-a can be prepared at the same time. The other fingers cannot be prepared at the beginning of the picking pattern. This means: for example, in the picking pattern p-a-m-i you can only prepare p and a. For a-m-i you can only prepare a (but keep p on the g-string in the pieces ahead.) And for p-i-a-m you can prepare p, i and a while m is on it's own.

The idea is to have your picking fingers touch strings to stabilize your picking hand, enabling you to play more relaxed and secure.

String contact is a direct result of preparation. It means a concious feeling of touching the string you're about to pluck with your finger.

Anchor finger is a finger that keeps fretting a certain note, while the chord around it changes and other fingers switch their position.

If you have a hard time keeping one finger on a fret while other fingers move try this:

Tap each finger of the chord onto its fret while the other fingers stay on.

Imagine your finger to grow roots into the fretboard. Then lift off the other fingers on at a time.

Guide finger is a finger that stays on the same string in a chord change. This finger slides along the string into the new position and the other fingers are placed subsequently for the new chord.

Führungsfinger bleiben beim Griffwechsel auf derselben Saite. Gleite mit diesem finger in die neue Position und setze die anderen Finger danach auf.

HOW TO PRACTICE

Practicing is a complex topic and whole books can be - and are! - filled with good advice on how to make the most of your time.

It's one of the few things, I'm convinced you cannot really learn from a book, but from a teacher who has years of experience in practicing. And then you still have to walk the road of development yourself.

What I find most important is, developing and maintaining awareness while practicing and cultivating positive emotions to go with your practice.

Willful automating of movements and active listening will lead you to productive and analytical practicing habits.

Positive emotions, a result of non-judgemental thoughts, are the basis for anything we want to happily keep doing. And let's be honest: we've all picked up the ukulele to HAVE FUN! So don't beat yourself up, if something isn't working immediately. Go explore and seek help when you need it. Catch me at a festival with my workshop on practicing techniques, book a lesson (with me or other people who you trust to have successfully practiced in their lives) and make sure to take your time with all of it.

GUTES ÜBEN

Das Thema Üben ist komplex und es könnten - und werden! - ganze Bücher mit guten Ratschlägen gefüllt, wie man Übezeit besonders effizient nutzt.

Üben gehört zu den wenigen Themen, bei denen ich davon überzeugt bin, dass man sie nicht von einem Buch, sondern eher von einer Lehrperson, die jahrelange Übeerfahrung hat, lernen kann.

Das Wichtigste für mich ist es, Bewusstheit beim Üben zu entwickeln und beizubehalten und dein Üben mit positiven Emotionen zu verbinden.

Bewusstes Automatisieren von Bewegungen und aktives Hören führen zu einem lösungsorientierten und analytischen Üben.

Positive Emotionen, meist das Ergebnis von nicht-bewertenden Gedanken, sind die Basis für alles Mögliche, was wir glücklich und zufrieden über einen langen Zeitraum machen wollen. Und wenn wir ehrlich sind, haben wir doch alle mit dem Ukulelespielen angefangen, weil wir SPAß HABEN wollten. Ärgere dich also nicht, wenn etwas nicht sofort klappt. Mach dich auf die Suche nach einer Lösung und hol' dir Hilfe wenn nötig. Vielleicht erwischst du ja meinen Workshop zum Thema Üben auf einem Ukulele Festival oder buche eine Unterrichtsstunde (bei mir oder bei jemand anderem, der schon erfolgreich über einen längeren Zeitraum geübt hat) und lass' dir vor allem mit allem Zeit.

DIE WICHTIGSTEN ÜBETIPPS FÜR DIESES BUCH

Jedem Musikstück in diesem Buch liegt ein spezifiisches Zupfmuster zugrunde. Du findest es rechts unter dem Titel des Stücks. Übe zunächst dieses Zupfmuster ohne Griffe, also auf leeren Saiten. Welche Saiten du dafür brauchst, siehst du in der Tabulatur. Ignoriere einfach die Zahlen und spiele die leeren Saiten mit den entsprechenden Fingern der Zupfhand. Manchmal ändern sich die Saiten im Verlauf der Etüde. Schau anfangs das ganze Stück durch und übe jede Position des Zupfmusters auf leeren Saiten.

Schnelles Tempo steht beim Üben grundsätzlich nicht im Vordergrund. Es gibt kein ‚zu langsam' beim Üben. Für die Stücke in diesem Buch ist mir wichtig, dass du sie vor allem musikalisch mit schönem Klang spielst, nicht möglichst schnell.

Es gibt allerdings eine sehr effektive Übung, wie du dein Spieltempo erhöhen kannst.

Sprinten: Spiele das Zupfmuster einmal sehr langsam und dann zweimal doppelt so schnell und wiederhole das eine ganze Weile lang, so dass du zwischen langsam und schnell abwechselst. Das langsame Tempo solltest du <u>sehr</u> langsam wählen, damit du das schnelle Tempo noch einigermaßen bewältigen kannst. Achte beim langsamen Teil darauf, alle Bewegungen zu kontrollieren und beobachte beim

MOST IMPORTANT PRACTICE TIPS FOR THIS BOOK

Every piece in this book is based on a specific picking pattern. You find it on the right hand side below the title. Practice this picking pattern on open strings before adding any fretting action. You can see the strings you'll need to use in the tabs of the piece. Just ignore the fret numbers and pick every string with the assigned finger of your picking hand. Sometimes you'll change strings over the course of the piece. Look at the whole piece and practice every picking hand position on open strings.

Fast tempo shouldn't be a high priority while practicing. There is no 'too slow' when you practice. I'd be much happier, if your priorities while playing my pieces would be to play them musically and with a nice sound, rather than super-fast. However, there is a nice and efficient exercise that will make your playing faster while hopefully keeping it comfortable.

Sprinting: Play the picking pattern once in a slow tempo and then twice douple speed. Then repeat that for a whole while going back and forth between slow and fast. You should choos a <u>very</u> slow tempo, to be able to successfully master the fast tempo. The slow part gives you a chance to concentrate on controlling every movement, while the fast part just allows you to observe what is already coming off. If you can't keep the technical level of the slow part, slow down the whole exercise until you can be precise in the fast part, as well.

You'll find more tips for your picking hand in

my book 'Pop & Rock Ukulele: Picking'.

For most pieces in this book it's also a good idea to practice your fretting hand independently from any picking pattern. The chord diagrams for each etude will help you with that. Try to find a comfortable fretting hand position for each note constellation in a diagram. Pick or strum the strings at the same time to find out how the chord sounds. Fret the chords at different spots or systematically move the chord up and down the fretboard. This will make you more flexible in approaching different chords and also will develop your fretting hand. Press fretted notes only as hard as necessary. This is easier said than done and as experience shows, you'll need to come back to letting go of excess pressure again and again. Frequently shake out your fretting hand while practicing. This will help you to get rid of accumulated tension, not letting it build over a long time.

And the most important practice rule of all: Go slow! Choose a tempo that allows you to control every aspects of your playing that you want to control. Here are some questions that might help you with your practicing: Do I like what I hear? Are all the notes equally loud? Are the melody notes louder than the rest? Am I consistent in my tempo? Do I have fun with the sound I hear?

schnellen Teil, wieviel du vom langsamen Teil übertragen kannst. Werde insgesamt langsamer, wenn du dauerhaft den schnellen Teil nicht bewältigst. In meinem Buch ‚Pop- und Rockukulele: Zupfmuster' findest du noch mehr Übetipps und Tricks für deine Zupfhand.

Am besten übst du bei den meisten Stücken die Greifhand separat. Dabei können dir die Griffbilder zu den Stücken helfen. Finde bequeme Positionen für die Griffe, die jeweils in einem Griffbild dargestellt sind. Schlage die Saiten unabhängig vom Zupfmuster gleichzeitig an, um einen schönen Gesamtklang zu finden. Baue die Griffe auch an anderen Stellen des Griffbretts auf oder verschiebe die Griffe über das Griffbrett. Das wird dich im Umgang mit den Griffen flexibler machen. Achte darauf, nur mit soviel Druck zu arbeiten, wie nötig. Das ist leichter gesagt, als getan und die Erfahrung zeigt, dass du dich immer wieder neu damit beschäftigen musst, überschüssige Spannung loszulassen. Schüttel deine Greifhand immer wieder gut aus. Das wird dir helfen, nicht zu viel Spannung aufzubauen.

Und die wichtigste Überegel: Mach' langsam! Spiele so langsam, dass du alle Aspekte deines Spiels, die du kontrollieren möchtest, auch kontrollieren kannst. Fragen, die dir beim Üben helfen sind: Gefällt mir, was ich höre? Sind alle Töne gleich laut? Sind die Melodietöne lauter, als die anderen? Bleibt das Tempo gleich? Macht mir der Klang Freude?

Repertoire

Tipps und Anmerkungen

Hier sind drei kurze Etüden, die deinen Daumen fit machen. Alle drei sollen nur mit dem Daumen p gespielt werden.

- Lege deinen m-Finger auf die a-Saite und lass ihn dort liegen. Deine Zupfhand wird dadurch stabiler.
- Sei von vornherein für die einzelnen gegriffenen Töne bereit. Lass deine Greifhand schon in der Nähe der Bünde.
- Achte darauf, den Rhythmus ganz richtig zu spielen.
- Hör dir die Audiodateien an und schau die Videos an.

Practice and Performance Notes

Here are three short etudes to get your thumb going. All three are designed to only be played with your thumb p.

- Place your m-Finger on the a-string and leave it there. That'll give your picking hand more stability.
- Be ready to fret the single notes with your fretting hand. Hover your hand close to the frets.
- Get the rhythm exactly right.
- Listen to the audio files and watch the videos.

01 Get Ready
fretting single notes / Einzeltöne greifen - p

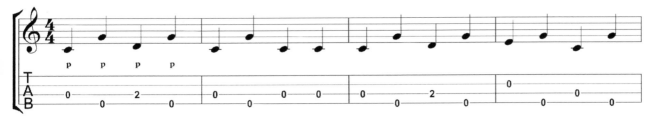

02 Waltzing around
3/4 time - fretting single notes / Einzeltöne greifen - 3/4-Takt - p

03 Rocking p
eighth notes - fretting single notes / Einzeltöne greifen- Achtelnoten - p

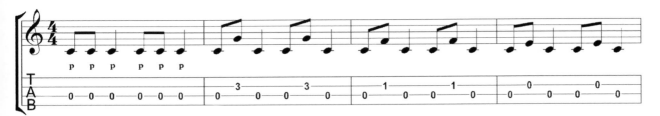

01 GET READY
fretting single notes / Einzeltöne greifen - p

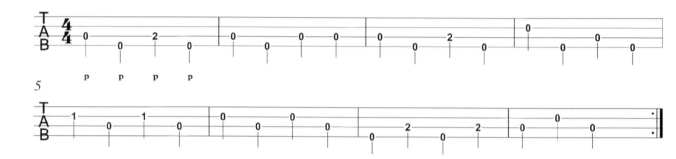

02 WALTZING AROUND
3/4 time - fretting single notes / Einzeltöne greifen - 3/4-Takt - p

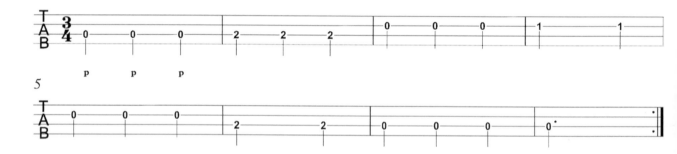

03 ROCKING P
eighth notes - fretting single notes / Einzeltöne greifen- Achtelnoten - p

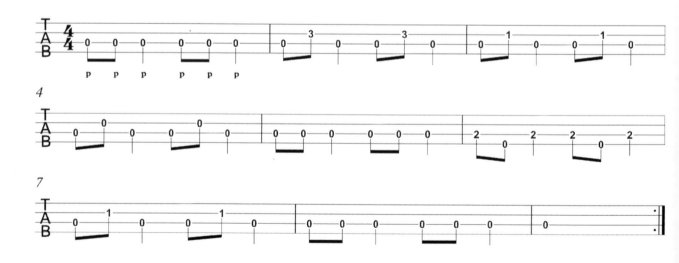

01 GET READY
fretting single notes / Einzeltöne greifen - p

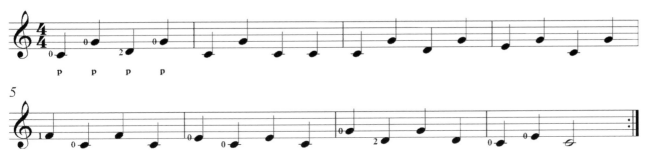

02 WALTZING AROUND
3/4 time - fretting single notes / Einzeltöne greifen - 3/4-Takt - p

03 ROCKING P
eighth notes - fretting single notes / Einzeltöne greifen- Achtelnoten - p

Tipps und Anmerkungen

Circle ist eine einfache Etüde für das Zupfmuster p-i.
Deine Greifhand muss sich dabei immer nur um einen gegriffenen
Ton kümmern.

- Lass Finger deiner Greifhand liegen, wo es geht (z.B. hebe den
  2. Finger nur für die leere Saite in den Takten 2 und 4 in der ersten Zeile des Stückes ab).
- Achte auf guten Saitenkontakt deiner Zupfhand.
- P und i entfernen sich im Verlauf des Stückes voneinander und
  spielen im größeren Abstand. Finde eine Handposition in der du
  beide Saiten spielen kannst, ohne die Hand bewegen zu müssen.

Practice and Performance Notes

Circle is an basic etude for developing your p-i picking, while your
fretting hand only takes care of one note at a time.

- Let fretting fingers stay on a note when possible (i.e. lift off 2nd
  finger only for the open string in bar 2 and 4 of the first line).
- Aim for good string contact in your picking hand.
- As p and i move further away from each other throughout the
  piece make sure to find a static position for your picking hand.

fretting positions for
2-4 bars in a row

Griffpositionen für
jeweils 2-4 Takte

04 CIRCLE
easy fretting - Einzeltöne greifen / p-i

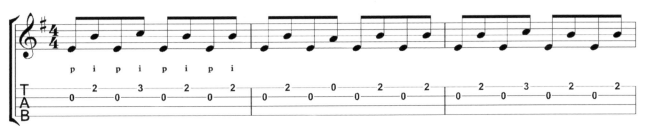

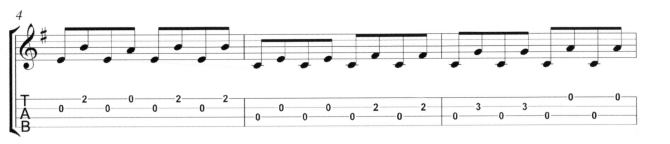

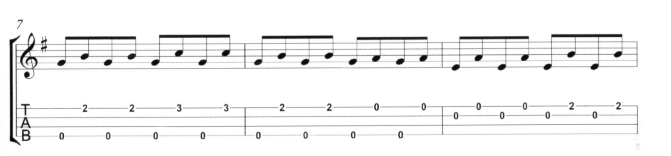

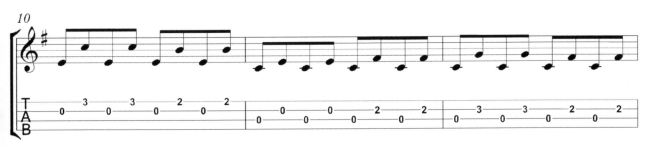

04 CIRCLE (TAB)

easy fretting - Einzeltöne greifen / p-i

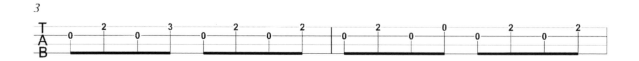

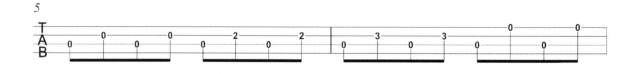

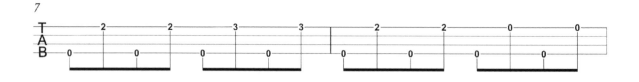

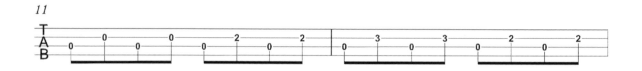

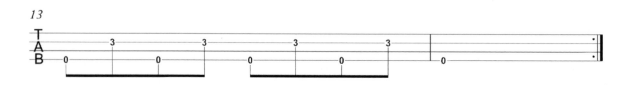

04 CIRCLE (NOTEN)

easy fretting - Einzeltöne greifen / p-i

Tipps und Anmerkungen

Sunny Morning ist eine einfache Etüde, die dein p-m Zupfmuster trainiert und dir Einzeltöne in höheren Lagen auf dem Griffbrett vermittelt.

- Halte deine Zupfhand so ruhig wie möglich.
- Arbeite daran, deine Finger einzeln zu bewegen, statt den ganzen Arm für die Zupfbewegung zu benutzen.
- Versuche nicht zu viel mit der Greifhand am Griffbrett entlang zu rutschen.
- In Takt 5 verwende den 1. Finger für das h' auf der E-Saite am 7. Bund.
- Fange in Takt 13 mit dem 3. Finger am 3. Bund an und greife dann den 2. Bund mit dem 2. Finger und den 1. Bund mit dem 1. Finger.
- Übe diese Etüde auch mit p-i.

Practice and Performance Notes

Sunny Morning is an easy etude that will train your p-m picking pattern and make you more familiar with single notes up the fretboard.

- Keep your picking hand very stable.
- Aim for individually moving your picking fingers rather than using your whole arm .
- Avoid sliding up and down the fretboard with your fretting hand too much.
- In bar 5 use your 1st finger for the B on the 7th fret of the E-string.
- In bar 13 start with your 3rd finger on the 3rd fret, then use your 2nd finger for the 2nd fret and your 1st finger for the 1st fret .
- Also practice this etude with p-i.

fretting positions for 4 bars in a row

Griffpositionen für jeweils 4 Takte

05 SUNNY MORNING
single notes in higher positions / Einzeltöne in höheren Lagen - p-m

05 Sunny Morning (Tab)
single notes in higher positions / Einzeltöne in höheren Lagen - p-m

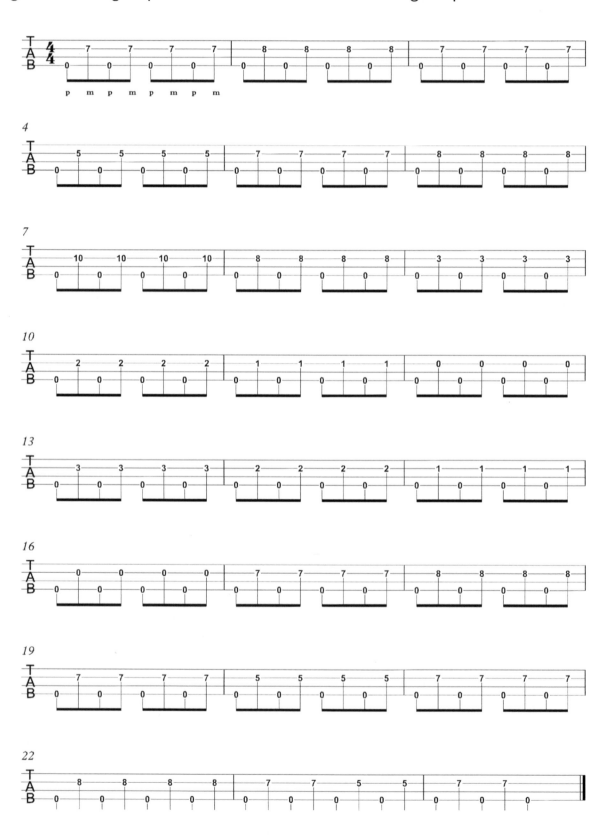

05 Sunny Morning (Noten)
single notes in higher positions / Einzeltöne in höheren Lagen - p-m

Tipps und Anmerkungen

Afternoon Light ist eine einfache Etüde für das Zupfmuster p-m.
Der Daumen p springt zwischen Saiten, während m immer auf der
a-Saite spielt.

- Finde eine Position für die Zupfhand, in der du jede Position
  von p spielen kannst.
- Halte die Zupfhand ruhig.
- Lass deine Greifhand über der nächsten Position schweben,
  während du leere Saiten spielst.
- Lass Finger deiner Greifhand liegen, wo sie liegen bleiben können.
- Suche nach längeren Passagen, an denen du Finger schon
  liegen lassen kannst, wie es in den letzten drei Griffbildern dargestellt ist.
- Streiche den letzten Akkord mit p.

Practice and Performance Notes

Afternoon Light is a Beginner's etude to help with your p-m picking
pattern. Your thumb p moves between different strings, while m
always picks the a-string.

- Find a picking hand position that allows you to play every
  thumb p position.
- Hold your picking hand still.
- Let your fretting hand hover above the next position while play-
  ing open strings.
- Keep notes fretted where possible.
- Go look for passages that allow you to fret more than one fin-
  ger; just like you can see in the last three chord diagrams.
- Strum the last chord with p.

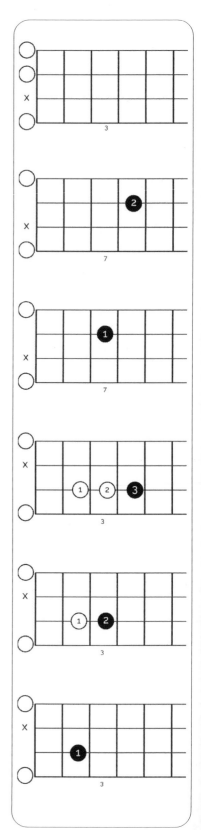

06 AFTERNOON LIGHT
chromatic melody - chromatische Melodie / p-m

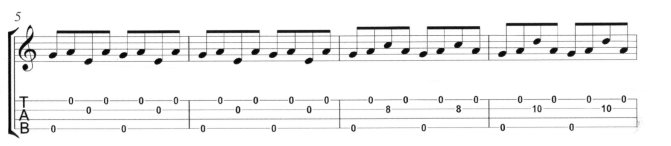

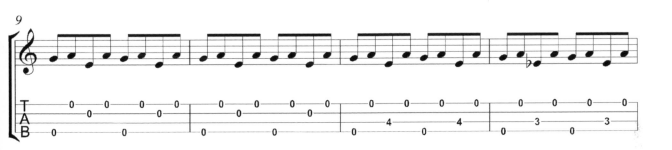

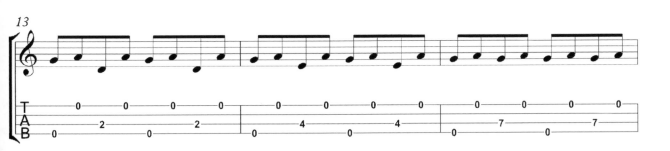

06 Afternoon Light (Tab)
chromatic melody - chromatische Melodie / p-m

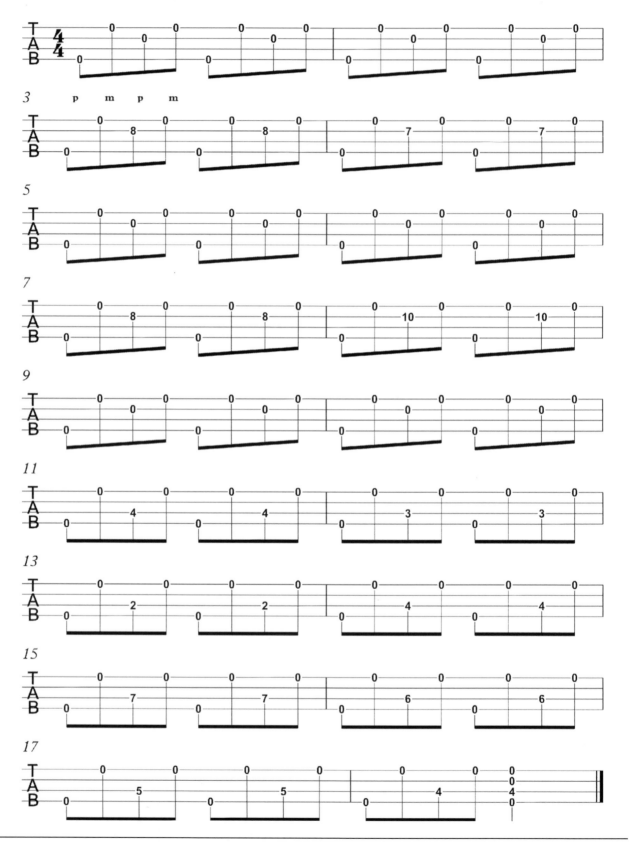

06 AFTERNOON LIGHT (NOTEN)
chromatic melody - chromatische Melodie / p-m

Tipps und Anmerkungen

Marching Back Home is eine einfache Etüde für dein p-i-p-m Zupfmuster.

- Greife alle Töne für jeweils zwei Takte (z.B. den 2. Bund auf der
  g-Saite und den 1. Bund auf der e-Saite - ein normaler F-Dur-
  Griff - für die ersten beiden Takte; dann den 2. Bund auf der
  g-Saite - ein Am-Griff - für die nächsten beiden Takte, usw.).
- Rutsche in Takt 7 mit dem 3. Finger zum 2. Bund (Führungsfinger), das erleichtert den Übergang zurück zum 1. Takt für die
  Wiederholung.
- Ab Takt 9 bewegt sich der Daumen p zwischen der c-Saite und
  der g-Saite.

Practice and Performance Notes

Marching Back Home is an easy etude to develop your
p-i-p-m picking pattern.

- Fret all the notes you need for two bars (i.e. g-string 2nd fret
  and e-string 1st fret - a regular F major chord - for the first two
  bars; g-string 2nd fret - a regular A minor chord - for the next
  two bars, etc.).
- In bar 7 slide down to the 2nd fret with your 3rd finger (guide
  finger), that will make the transition back to bar 1 for the repeti-
  tion a lot easier.
- From bar 9 onwards your thumb p moves between the c-string
  and the g-string.

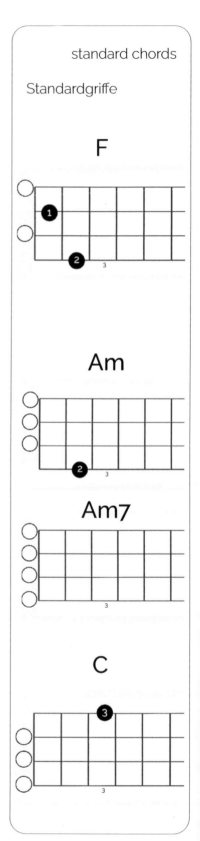

07 Marching Back Home

p changing strings - guide finger / Saitenwechsel mit p - Führungsfinger / p-i-p-m

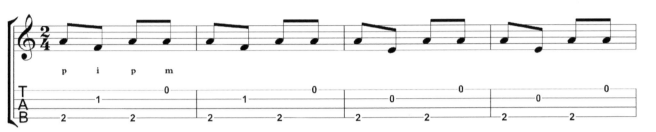

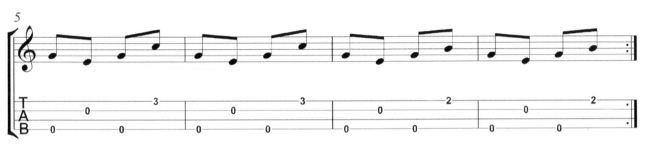

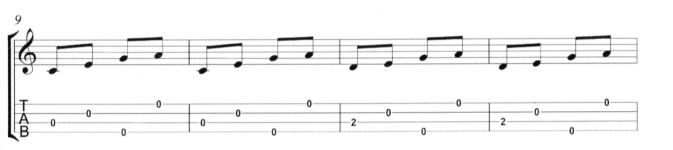

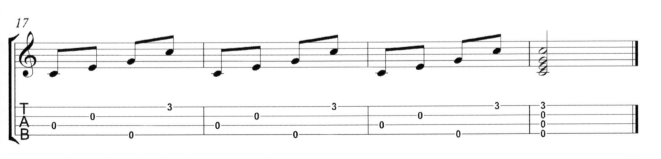

07 MARCHING BACK HOME (TAB)
p changing strings - guide finger / Saitenwechsel mit p - Führungsfinger / p-i-p-m

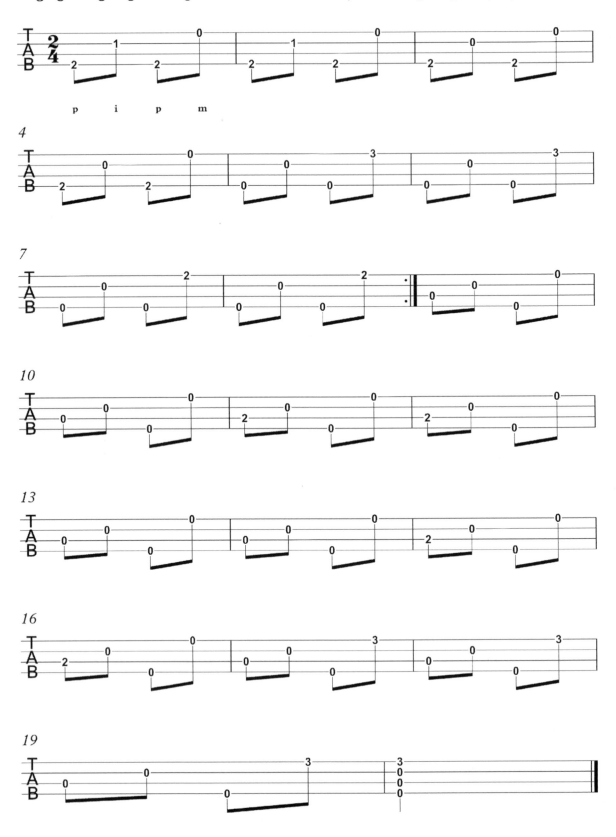

07 Marching Back Home (Noten)

p changing strings - guide finger / Saitenwechsel mit p - Führungsfinger / p-i-p-m

Tipps und Anmerkungen

Circle Dance ist eine fortgeschrittene Etüde, die Lagenwechsel
trainiert. Der Daumen p zupft eine Saite, während der i-Finger über
zwei Saiten Töne anschlägt (Up-Strum / Aufschlag).

- Entspanne dein erstes Fingerglied im i-Finger - das wird es dir
  einfacher machen, eine stabile Handposition zu finden und zu
  halten.
- Fange sehr langsam an - das Stück wird von selbst schneller.
- Die meisten Töne werden in einer Kombination aus 1-2 oder
  1-3 gegriffen. In Takt 12 springst du zum 8. und zum 10. Bund.
  Greife den 8. Bund mit dem 2. Finger und den 10. Bund mit dem
  4. Finger. Du brauchst nämlich gleich danach den 1. Finger auf
  dem 7. Bund.
- Werde am Ende sehr viel langsamer (das bezeichnet man als
  ‚ritardando' = rit.) und strumme den letzten Klang mit dem i-Finger aufwärts von der a- zur g-Saite.
- Übe die Etüde auch mit p-m.

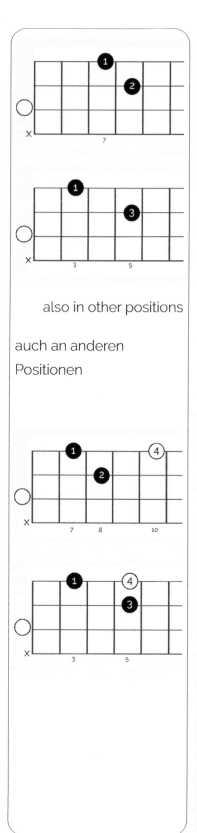

also in other positions

auch an anderen
Positionen

Practice and Performance Notes

Circle Dance is an advanced etude that develops your ability to
shift to different positions across the fingerboard and combines
picking with an up-strum.

- Relax first finger joint in i-Finger, that'll make it easier to find a
  static hand position for your picking hand.
- Start very slow as the piece will speed up later.
- Most notes are fretted either 1-2 or 1-3. In bar 12 you jump up
  to the 8th and 10th fret. Use your 2nd finger on the 8th fret and
  your 4th finger on the 10th fret, as you'll need your 1st finger on
  the 7th fret a moment later.
- Slow down significantly towards the end (that's called 'ritardando' = rit.) of the piece and strum the last note upward with i.
- Practice this etude also with p-m.

08 Circle Dance

3rd intervals / shifts - Terzen / Lagenwechsel / p-i (i-strum)

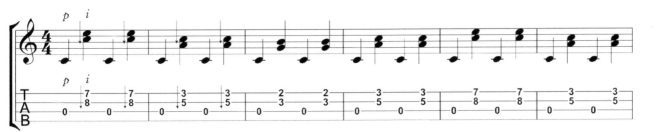

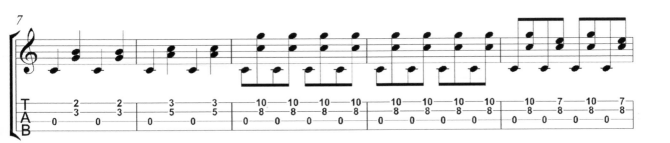

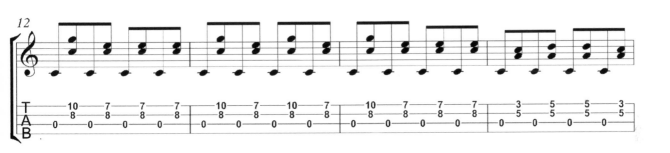

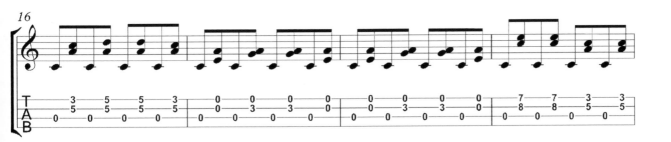

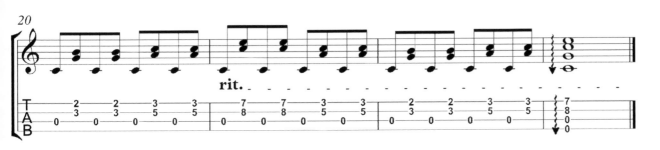

08 CIRCLE DANCE (TAB)
3rd intervals / shifts - Terzen / Lagenwechsel / p-i (i-strum)

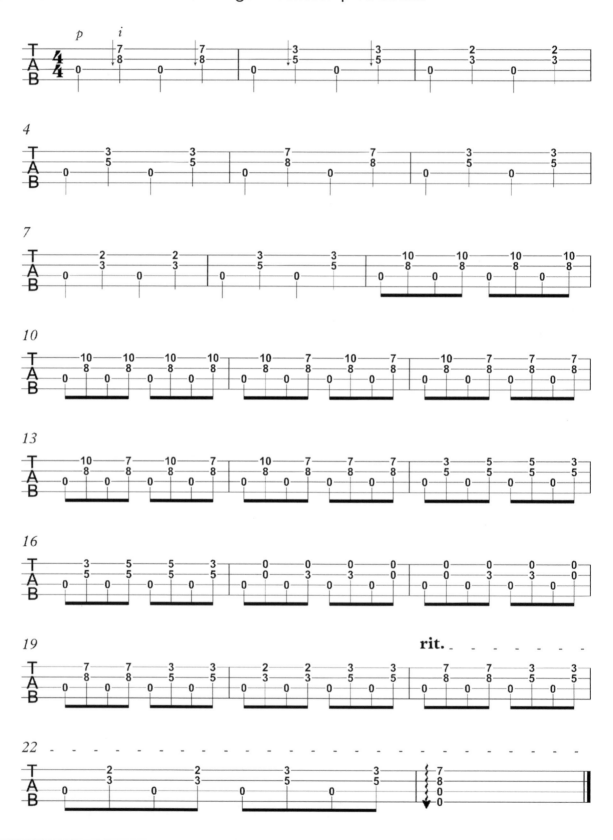

08 Circle Dance (Noten)

3rd intervals / shifts - Terzen / Lagenwechsel / p-i (i-strum)

Tipps und Anmerkungen

Evening Lullaby ist eine ruhige Etüde, die das Zupfuster pm-i entwickelt. Deine Greifhand greift meist zwei Töne auf unterschiedlichen Saiten im Abstand verschiedener Sext-Intervalle.

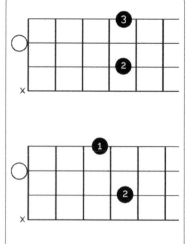

- Spiel langsam! - Es kommen noch fortgeschrittene Etüden für
  pm-i. Spiel diese hier möglichst ruhig und entspannt.
- Wie du siehst, zupfst du immer die gleichen drei Saiten. Du
  kannst deine Hand also ganz ruhig halten.
- Sextgriffe für die Greifhand kommen oft auch in anderen Kon-
  texten vor (z.B. in anderen Stücken oder beim Improvisieren).
  Wenn du sie jetzt bequem übst und gut verinnerlichst, wirst du
  dich lange an ihnen freuen können.

also in other positions

auch an anderen
Positionen

Practice and Performance Notes

Evening Lullaby is a calm etude to develop your pm-i picking. Your
fretting hand frets two strings at a time going in 6th intervals.

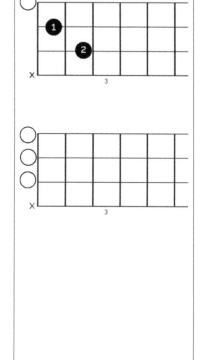

- Play it slow! - There are more advanced pm-i Etudes coming
  up, so be sure, you're able to play this calmly and in a relaxed
  way.
- Note that the picking hand always stays on the same three
  strings
- The fretting hand positions that are used here are pretty standard. You'll find them in other pieces, as well as solos. So make
  them comfortable and you'll be able to use them frequently
  and build on them later on.

09 Evening Lullaby
6th intervals - Sexten / pm-i

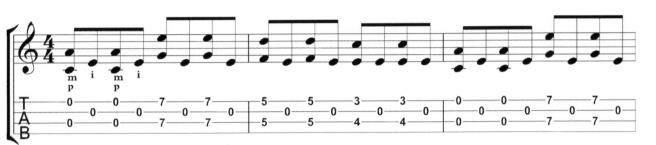

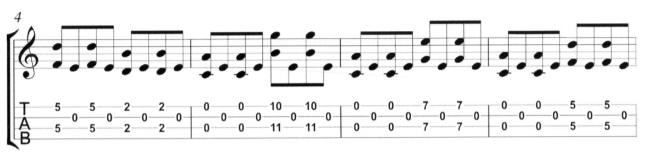

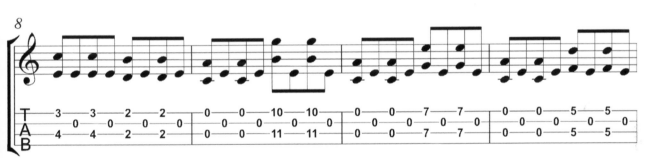

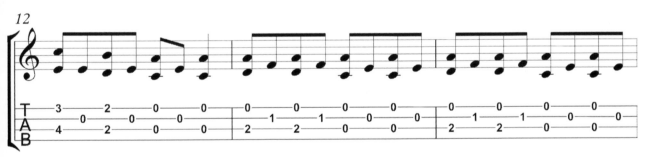

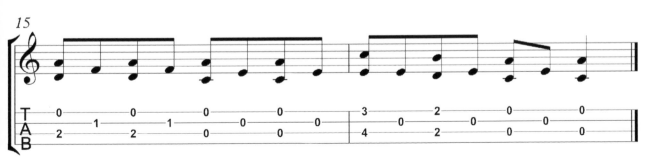

09 EVENING LULLABY (TAB)

6th intervals - Sexten / pm-i

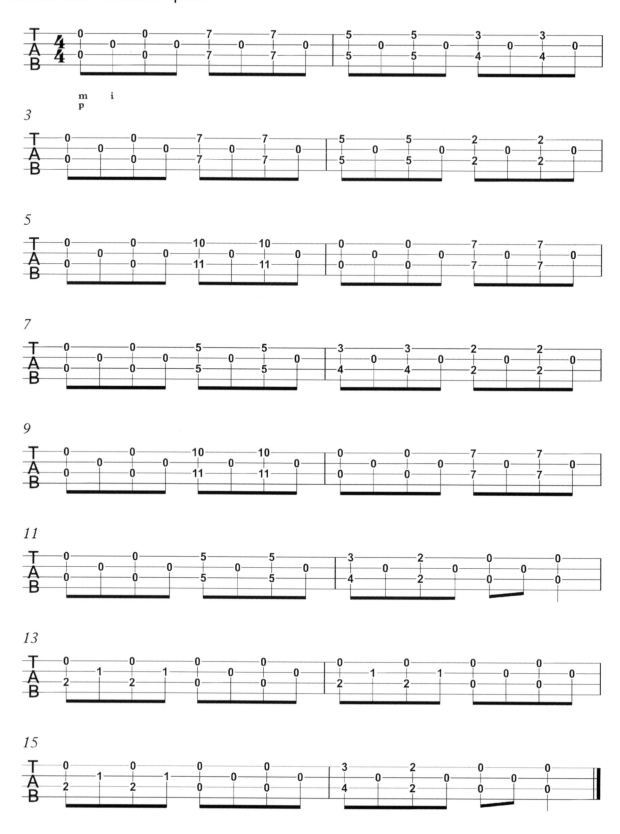

09 Evening Lullaby (Noten)
6th intervals - Sexten / pm-i

Tipps und Anmerkungen

Spring Lullaby ist eine pm-i Etüde, mit der du die Grundakkorde in höheren Lagen übst.

- Der Daumen p bewegt sich zwischen c- und g-Saite
- Übe Griffwechsel unabhängig vom Zupfmuster (vor allem den Griffwechsel von Takt 6 auf Takt 7).
- Ab Takt 13 werden den Grundakkorden noch Einzeltöne hinzugefügt. Lass den Grundgriff liegen und greife dann die einzelnen Töne zusätzlich.
- Mach langsam!

Practice and Performance Notes

Spring Lullaby is an intermediate pm-i Etude that also develops your basic chords in positions up the fretboard.

- Note that your thumb p is moving between the c- and the g-string.
- Practice challenging chord changes independently from the picking pattern (especially the chord change from bars 6 to 7).
- From bar 13 onwards single notes are added to the basic chord. Be sure to keep your chord while changing notes.
- Go slow!

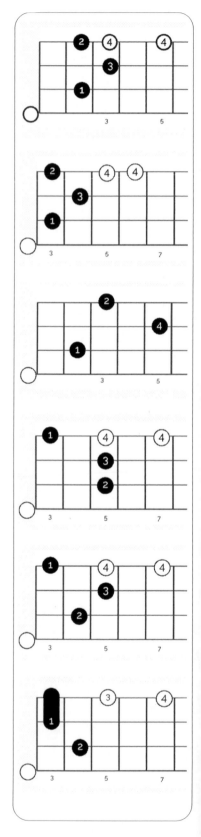

10 SPRING LULLABY

basic chords in higher positions - Grundakkorde in höheren Lagen / pm-i

10 SPRING LULLABY (TAB)
basic chords in higher positions - Grundakkorde in höheren Lagen / pm-i

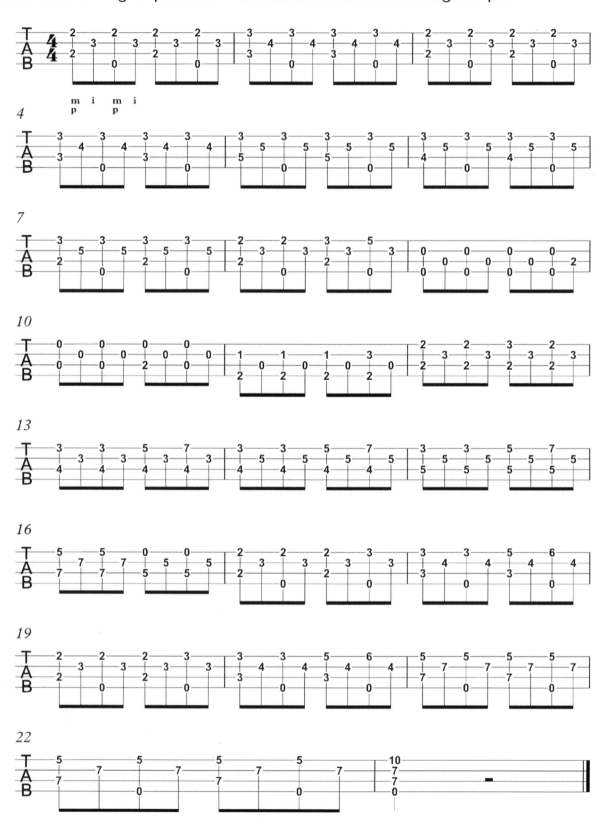

10 SPRING LULLABY (NOTEN)
basic chords in higher positions - Grundakkorde in höheren Lagen / pm-i

Tipps und Anmerkungen

Running Water soll als pm-i Etüde flüssige Leichtigkeit in dein Zupfmuster bringen. Deine Greifhand hält manche Töne und greift andere Töne manchmal zusätzlich.

- Wie du siehst, zupfst du immer die gleichen drei Saiten.
- Die Melodie springt von der g-Saite zur a-Saite und zurück.
- Greife die Töne, die du halten musst mit 1 und 2 (z.B. die Töne auf dem 5. Bund in den ersten Takten) und verwende deinen 3. und 4. Finger für andere Töne, wie die am 7. Bund im Takt 3).
- Tappe den letzten Ton (d auf der c-Saite am 2. Bund) mit dem i-Finger (sozusagen als Hammer-On), während du den vorherigen Griff weiter hältst.

Practice and Performance Notes

Running Water is a pm-i etude that aims for fluidity and lightness in your picking pattern. Your fretting hand holds static chords with some additional notes.

- Note how you're picking the same three strings thoughout the piece.
- The melody jumps from the g-string to the a-string and back.
- Fret your static chords (for example the note on the 5th fret through out the first bars) with 1 and 2 and use your fingers 3 and 4 to add notes like the 7th fret in bar 3).
- Tap the last note (d on c-string, 2nd fret) with your i-finger as a hammer-on, while holding the previous chord.

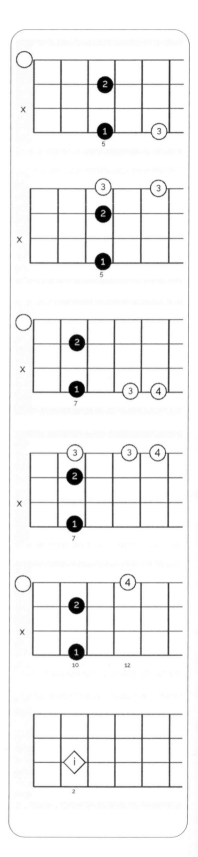

11 RUNNING WATER
melody moves to different string - Melodie wechselt Saiten / pm-i

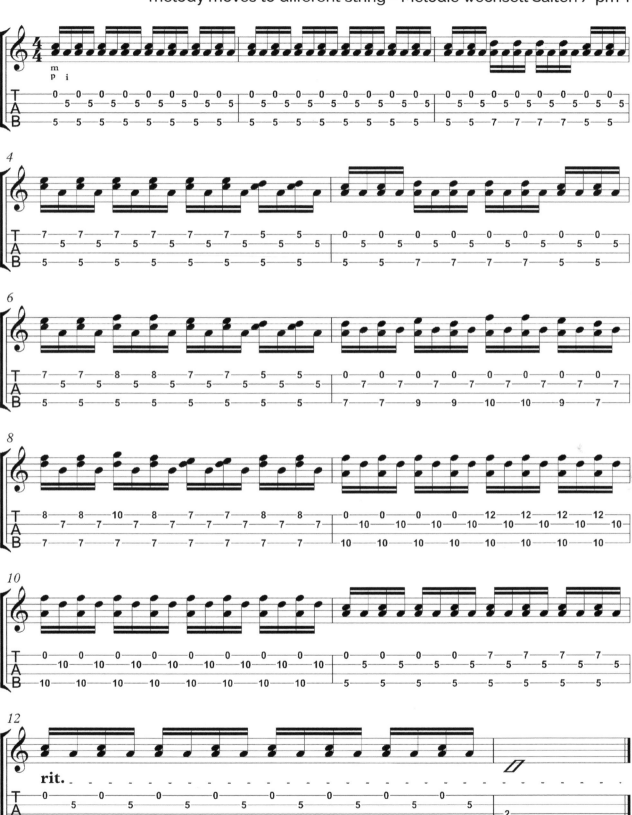

11 RUNNING WATER (TAB)

melody moves to different string - Melodie wechselt Saiten / pm-i

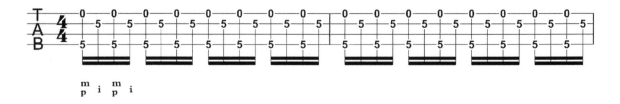

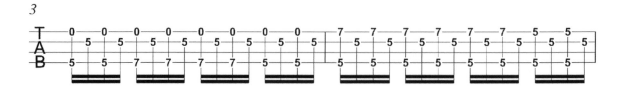

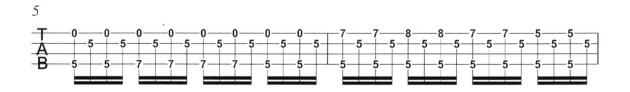

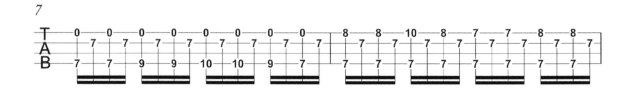

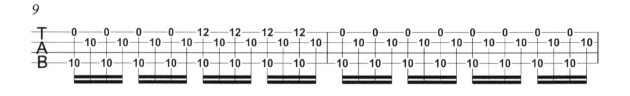

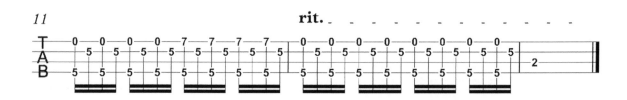

11 Running Water (Noten)

melody moves to different string - Melodie wechselt Saiten / pm-i

Tipps und Anmerkungen

French Carousel ist ein kleiner Walzer im 3/4-Takt, mit dem du an
deinem a-m-i Zupfmuster arbeiten kannst. Außerdem übst du mit
der Greifhand die Melodietöne lange auszuhalten und während-
dessen weitere Töne zu spielen.

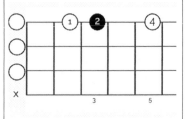

- Stütze deinen Daumen p auf die g-Saite und lasse ihn dort liegen. Das wird deiner Zupfhand viel Stabilität geben.
- Halte jeden gegriffenen Melodieton (z.B. das c auf der a-Saite am 3. Bund) so lange, bis du den nächsten Melodieton im
  nächsten Takt anschlägst.
- Versuche die Melodie herauszuarbeiten, indem du a laut und m
  und i etwas leiser spielst.
- Spiel ganz sanft!

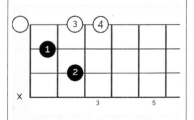

Practice and Performance Notes

French Carousel is a short waltz in 3/4 time. It's also an etude to
work on your a-m-i picking and your fretting hand's ability to hold
the melody while playing other notes.

- Put your thumb p on the g-string and keep it there. That'll give
  your picking hand a lot of stability.
- Be sure to hold every fretted melody note (i.e. c on the a-string
  / 3rd fret in bar 1), so it'll ring until you play the next melody
  note in the next bar.
- Try to bring out the melody notes by playing a loud and m and i
  a bit softer.
- Play gently!

12 FRENCH CAROUSEL

holding melody notes - Melodietöne halten / a-m-i

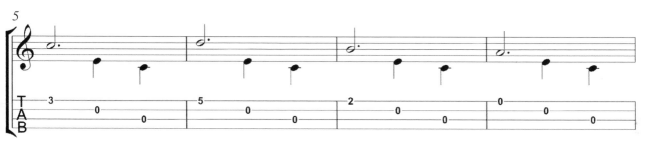

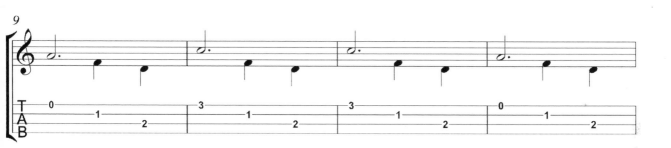

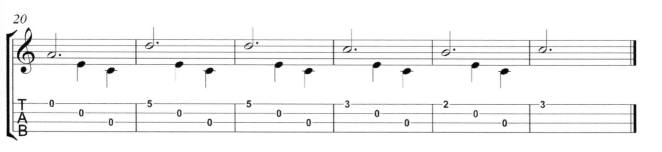

12 FRENCH CAROUSEL (TAB)
holding melody notes - Melodietöne halten / a-m-i

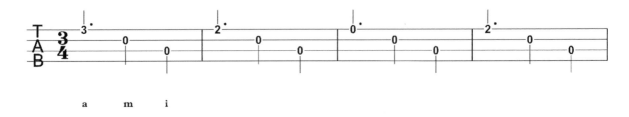

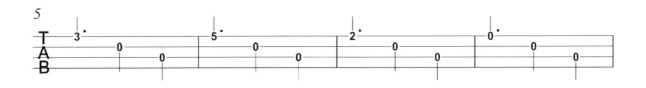

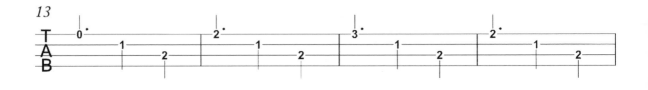

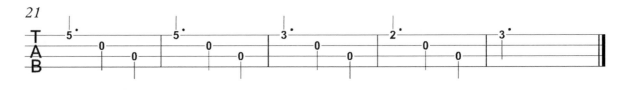

12 FRENCH CAROUSEL (NOTEN)
holding melody notes - Melodietöne halten / a-m-i

Tipps und Anmerkungen

Sinister Fog ist eine Etüde im mittleren Tempo für das Zupfmuster a-m-i. Für die Greifhand gibt es viele gute Fingersätze. Entscheide dich für einen Fingersatz, den du in die Noten einträgst und halte dich an diesen Fingersatz. Meinen Vorschlag siehst du in den Griffbildern und den Noten.

- Lasse alle Töne solange wie möglich klingen.
- In Takt 8 würde ich für den Ton am 5. Bund den 2. Finger vorschlagen. Das schafft günstige Voraussetzungen für die kommenden Takte.
- Der letzte Ton ist ein Flageolett auf der a-Saite am 12. Bund: ‚greife' den Ton direkt über dem Bundstäbchen; lass' deinen Finger einfach auf der Saite liegen und drücke die Saite nicht auf das Griffbrett herunter. Zupfe dann relativ stark die Saite an und hebe deinen Finger in aller Ruhe von der Saite ab. Wenn du die richtige Stelle erwischt hast, sollte ein glockenähnlicher Ton erklingen.

Practice and Performance Notes

Sinister Fog is a medium speed etude to develop your a-m-i Picking. There are many good ways to fret this etude. I'd suggest that you actively decide on a fretting hand fingering, write that into the music and stick to it. You can see my suggestions in the chord diagrams and the music.

- Let all the notes ring out as long as possible.
- In bar 8 I'd suggest you fret the note on the 5th fret with your 2nd finger. That will set you up for the bars to come.
- The last note is a harmonic on the 12th fret on the a string: 'fret' the note directly above the fretwire; let your finger rest on the string and don't press down. Pick quite hard and then slowly lift of your finger. If you've hit the right spot, a bell-like sound should ring out.

fretting positions for 4 bars in a row

Griffpositionen für jeweils 4 Takte

13 SINISTER FOG
shifts - Lagenwechsel / a-m-i

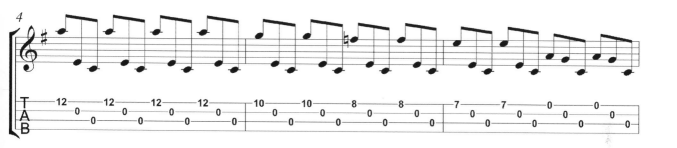

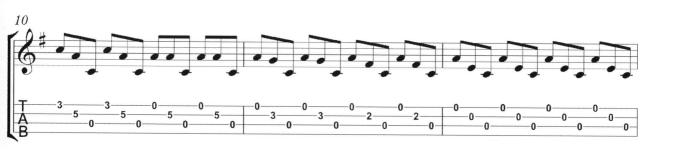

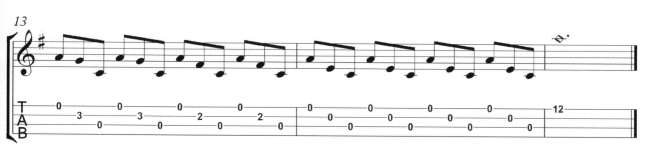

13 SINISTER FOG (TAB)

shifts - Lagenwechsel / a-m-i

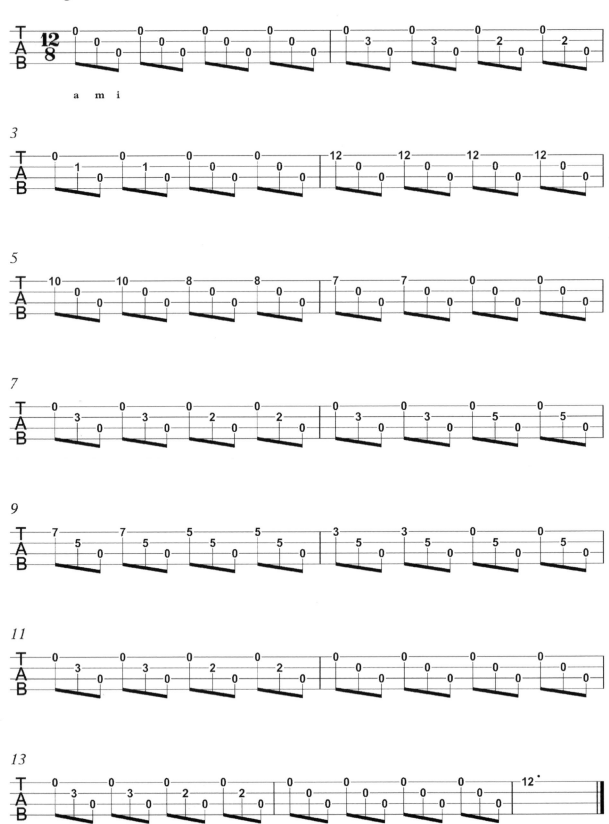

13 SINISTER FOG (NOTEN)
shifts - Lagenwechsel / a-m-i

Tipps und Anmerkungen

Hidden Treasure ist eine mittelschwere Etüde im 3/4-Takt. Die Melodie ist im Zupfmuster verborgen und wird immer mit dem a-Finger angeschlagen. Das Bild zeigt die Melodietöne der ersten beiden Takte eingekreist.

- Stütze deinen Daumen p auf die g-Saite und lasse ihn dort liegen. Das gibt deiner Zupfhand Stabilität.
- Halte gegriffene Melodietöne lange genug.
- Höre immer auf die Melodie!.

Practice and Performance Notes

Hidden Treasure is an intermediate etude in 3/4 time. The melody is hidden inside the picking pattern. You always pick it with your a-finger. I've circled the melody notes in bar 1 & 2 for you.

- Put your thumb p on the g-string and keep it there. This will give your picking hand a lot of stability.
- If you fret a melody note, be sure to hold it long enough.
- Always listen for the melody!

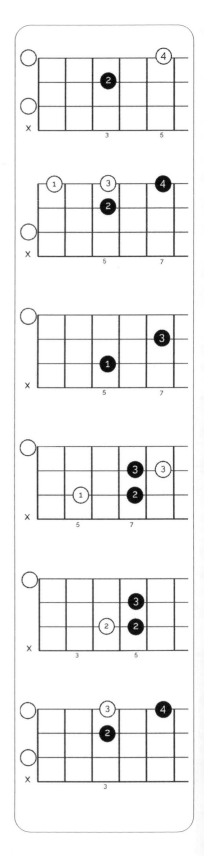

14 Hidden Treasure

hidden melody - verborgene Melodie/a-m-i-m-a-m

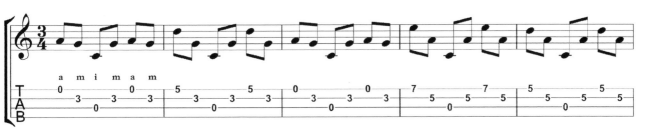

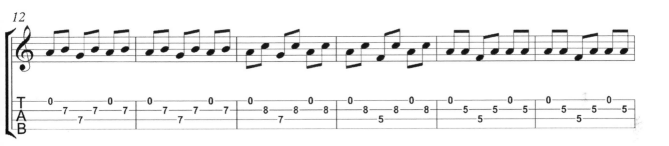

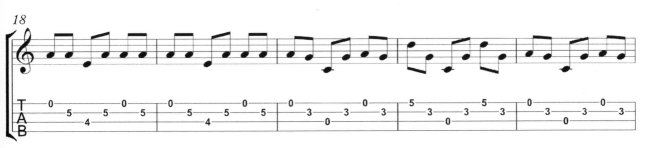

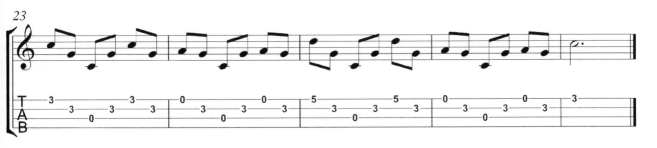

14 HIDDEN TREASURE (TAB)
hidden melody - verborgene Melodie/a-m-i-m-a-m

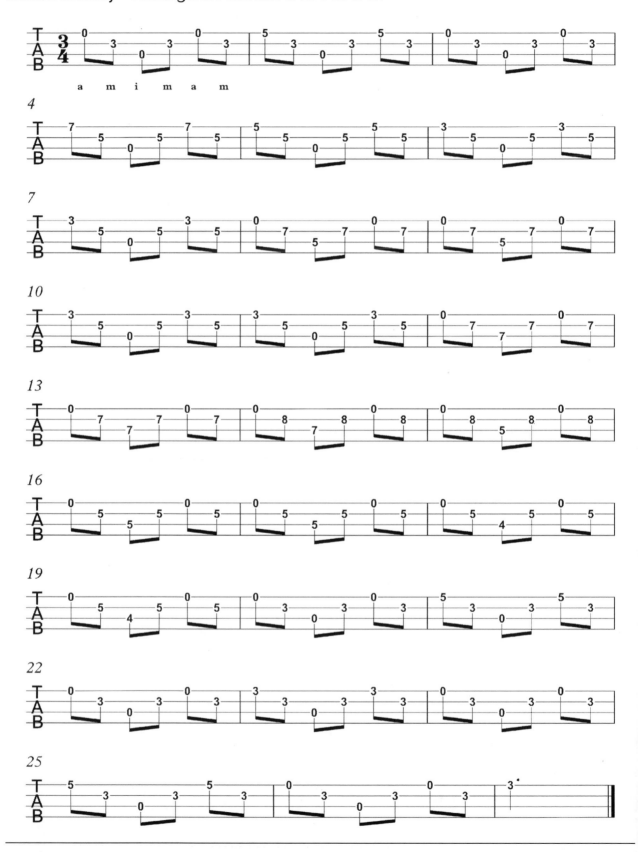

14 HIDDEN TREASURE (NOTEN)

hidden melody - verborgene Melodie/a-m-i-m-a-m

Tipps und Anmerkungen

Mit der Etüde Rocking the Boat trainierst du, verschiedene Finger für ganz unterschiedliche Aufgaben zu verwenden.

- Spüre mit dem a-Finger immer gut die Saite, bevor du sie an-schlägst (Saitenkontakt).
- Spiele die Einzelnote lauter als den Akkord.
- Achte darauf, die drei Akkordtöne immer gleichzeitig zu spielen.
- Arbeite in Takt 9 und den folgenden Takten daran, das c auf der a-Saite zu halten, währen du den Akkord abhebst und wieder auflegst.
- Übe den Akkord in Takt 14 separat und mache ihn so bequem wie möglich, bevor du ihn wieder in das ganze Stück einfügst.
- Den letzten Akkord kannst du strummen oder zupfen.

Practice and Performance Notes

Rocking the Boat is an etude that trains you to use different fingers for different tasks.

- Always feel the a-finger on the string before picking it (string contact).
- Play the single notes louder than the chords.
- Aim for playing all three notes of the chord at the same time.
- In bar 9 and the following bars, work on holding the c on the a-string while lifting off the chord and putting the chord back down.
- Practice the chord in bar 14 on its own for a bit and make it as comfortable as possible before putting it back into the piece.
- The last chord can be strummed or picked.

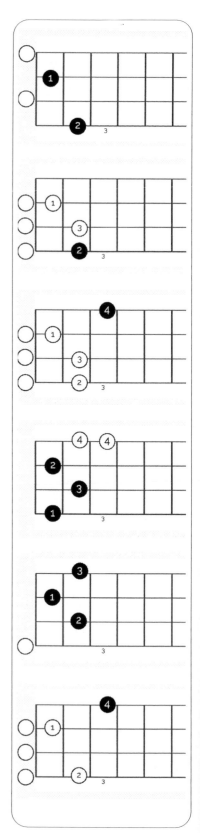

15 ROCKING THE BOAT

holding notes over chord movement - Einzeltöne über Akkordwechsel halten/a-mip

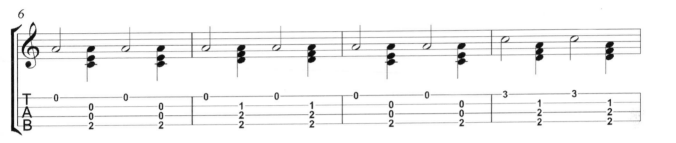

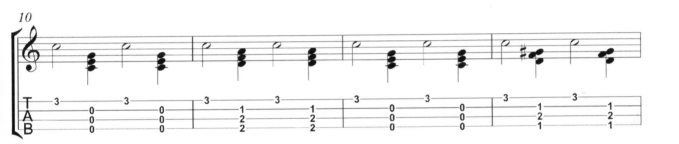

15 ROCKING THE BOAT (TAB)
holding notes over chord movement - Einzeltöne über Akkordwechsel halten/a-mip

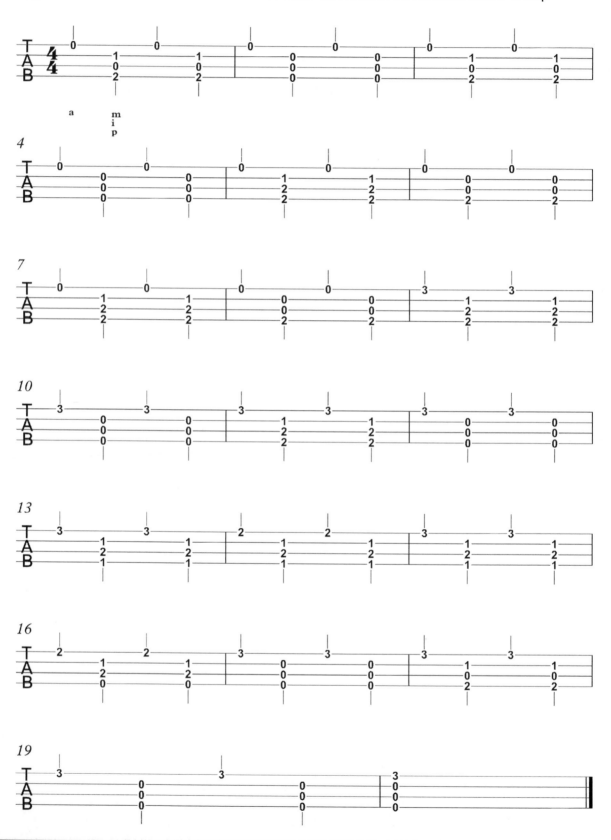

15 Rocking the Boat (Noten)

holding notes over chord movement - Einzeltöne über Akkordwechsel halten/a-mip

Tipps und Anmerkungen

Spring Dance ist ein Stück das ganz leicht und flink klingen soll.
Das Zupfmuster a-mip bleibt die ganze Etüde über gleich, sodass
deine Zupfhand ganz stabil bleiben kann.

*   Spüre mit dem a-Finger immer gut die Saite, bevor du sie an-
    schlägst (Saitenkontakt).
*   Spiele die Einzelnote lauter als den Akkord.
*   Versuche die drei Akkordtöne immer gleichzeitig zu spielen.
*   Greife die Töne am 5. Bund mit deinem 2. (c-Seite) und 3. (e-Sai-
    te) Finger und verankere sie gut am Griffbrett.
*   Verwende deinen 1. und 4. Finger für die zusätzlichen Melodie-
    töne.

Practice and Performance Notes

Spring Dance is a very light and swift piece. The picking pattern
a-mip stays throughout the whole etude, so your picking hand can
be very stable.

*   Always feel the a-finger on the string before picking it (string
    contact).
*   Play the single notes louder than the chords.
*   Aim for playing all three notes of the chord at the same time.
*   Fret the notes on the 5th fret with your 2nd (c-string) and 3rd
    (e-string) Finger and anchor them well.
*   Use your 1st and 4th finger for the added melody notes.

16 SPRING DANCE

anchoring fingers - Finger ankern / a-mip

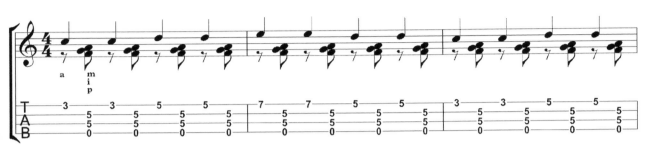

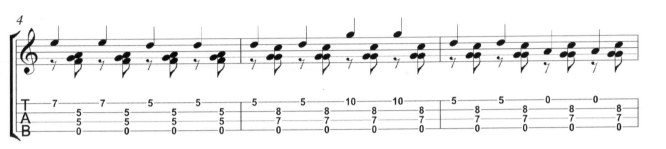

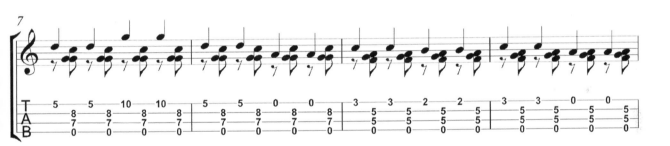

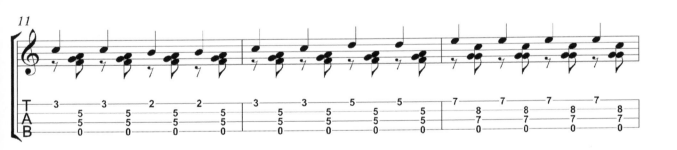

16 SPRING DANCE (TAB)

anchoring fingers - Finger ankern / a-mip

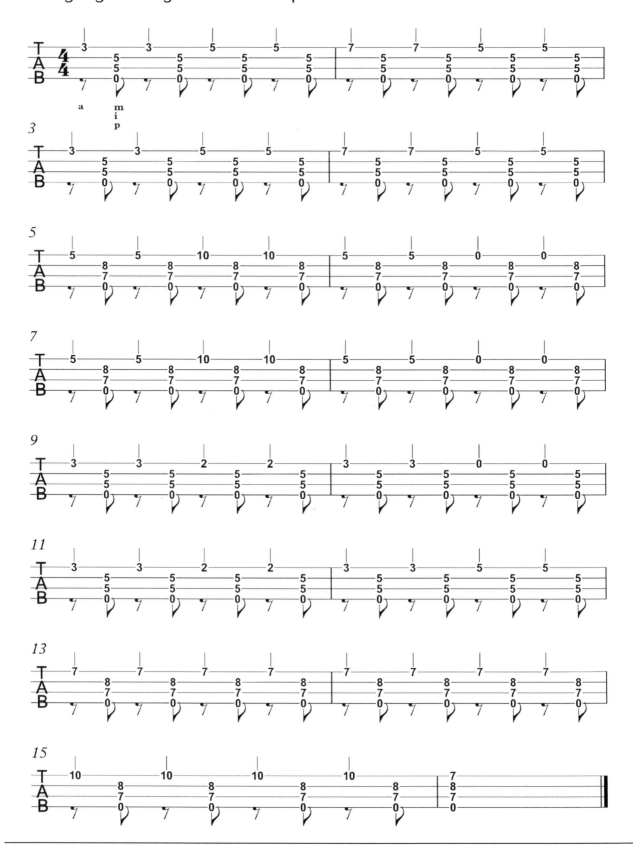

16 SPRING DANCE (NOTEN)
anchoring fingers - Finger ankern / a-mip

Tipps und Anmerkungen

Die Etüde Starry Horizon übt dein i-m-a-m Zupfmuster und die Stabilität deiner Zupfhand. Außerdem macht sie dich mit den hohen Lagen vertrauter.

- Stütze deinen Daumen p auf die g-Saite für mehr Stabilität.
- Dein 2. Finger greift immer auf der c-Saite und gleitet an ihr entlang in neue Positionen.
- Daraus ergeben sich Kombinationen mit entweder dem 1. Finger oder dem 3. Finger auf der e-Saite.
- Gelegentlich greift der 4. Finger einen Ton auf der a-Saite.
- Der 4. Finger greift in der vorletzten Zeile das e auf der a-Saite am 7. Bund. Verankere den Finger gut für die Griffwechsel.
- Isoliere jeden Takt, der dir kompliziert erscheint und beschäftige dich mit ihm bis er bequem ist. Füge erst danach das Stück wieder zusammen.

Practice and Performance Notes

Starry Horizon is an etude that will train your i-m-a-m picking pattern, as well as your picking hand stability. It'll also make you more comfortable with high positions on the fretboard.

- Place your thumb p on the g-string and keep it there for stability.
- Your 2nd finger always frets on the c-string and slides along it throughout the piece.
- With your 2nd finger on the c-string you get combinations with either the 1st or the 3rd finger on the e-string.
- Occasionally your 4th finger frets a note on the a-string.
- In the fourth line of the piece your 4th finger is fretting the e on the a-string/7th fret. Be sure to anchor the finger well, while changing the chords.
- Isolate any bar that is tricky and get comfortable with it before playing through the piece.

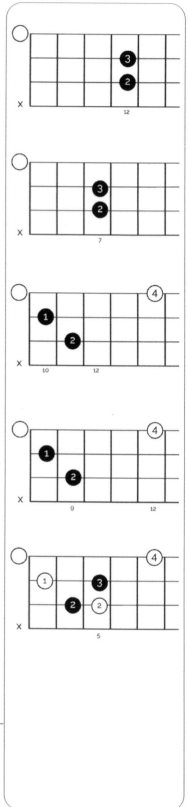

17 STARRY HORIZON

anchor and leading fingers - Anker- und Führungsfinger / i-m-a-m

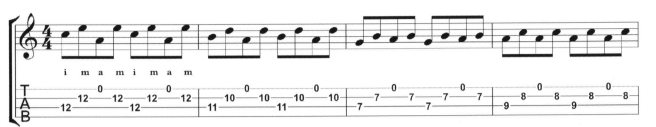

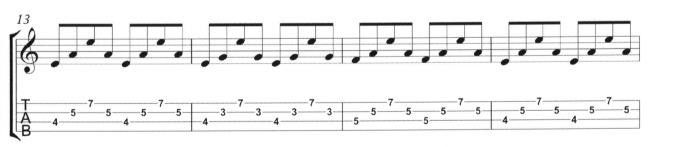

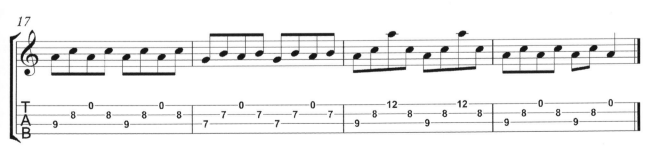

17 STARRY HORIZON (TAB)
anchor and leading fingers - Anker- und Führungsfinger / i-m-a-m

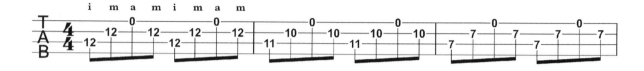

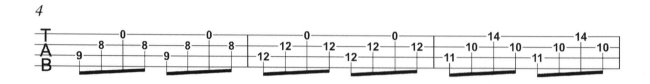

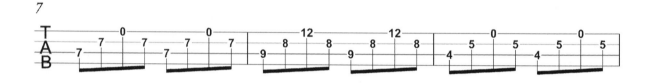

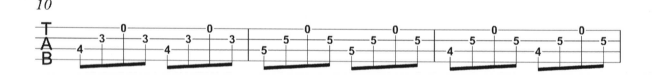

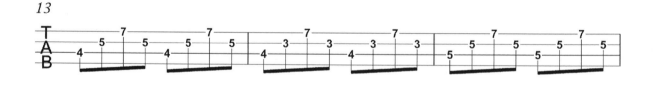

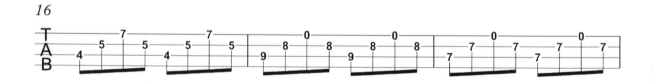

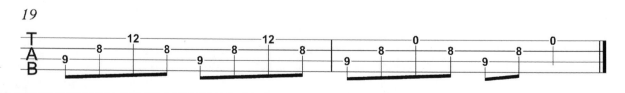

17 STARRY HORIZON (NOTEN)

anchor and leading fingers - Anker- und Führungsfinger / i-m-a-m

Tipps und Anmerkungen

No Time For a Chat entwickelt dein i-m-a-m Zupfmuster und soll
es bequem und flüssig machen.

- Stütze deinen Daumen p auf die g-Saite für mehr Stabilität.
- Suche nach Anker- und Führungsfingern; in beinahe jedem Ak-
  kordwechsel kannst du entweder einen Ankerfinger oder einen
  Führungsfinger zur Stabilisierung benutzen.
- Suche nach den kürzesten Wegen zwischen den Akkorden.
- Spiele die leere e-Saite in den Takten 14 und 16 leise, sodass
  sie sich in den Gesamtklang einfügt.

Practice and Performance Notes

No Time For a Chat is an etude that develops your i-m-a-m picking
pattern and aims for it to be comfortable and fluent.

- Place your thumb p on the g-string and keep it there for stability.
- Look for anchor and guiding fingers; for most chord changes you
  can either use an anchor finger or a guiding finger for stabilty.
- Look for the most direct connection between chords.
- Aim for playing the open e-string in bars 14 and 16 softly, to
  make it fit into the general sound of the chord.

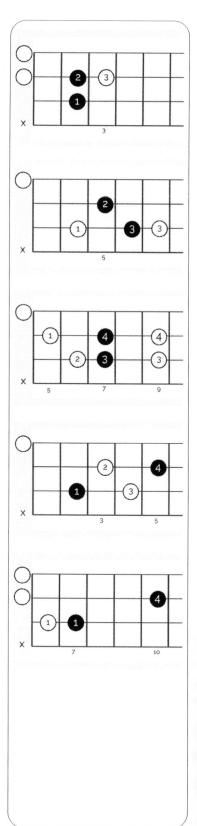

18 NO TIME FOR A CHAT

anchor and guiding fingers - Anker- und Führungsfinger / i-m-a-m

18 No Time For a Chat (Tab)

anchor and guiding fingers - Anker- und Führungsfinger / i-m-a-m

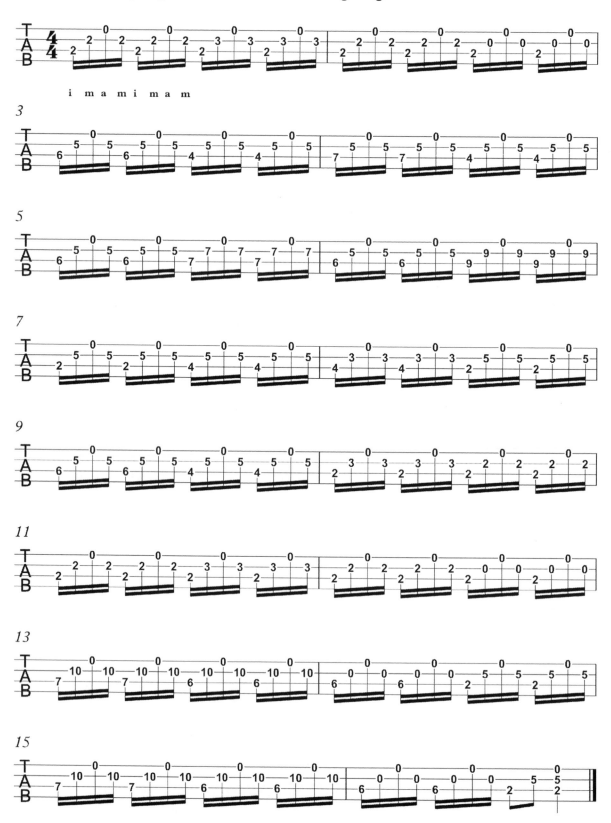

18 No Time For a Chat (Noten)

anchor and guiding fingers - Anker- und Führungsfinger / i-m-a-m

Tipps und Anmerkungen

Beneath The Surface ist eine ruhige Etüde, in deren Fokus das Zupfmuster p-a-m-i steht. Für die Greifhand ist vor allem das Konzept der Führungsfinger allgegenwärtig und in der zweiten Hälfte kannst du dich auf deine Barré-Technik über zwei bzw. drei Saiten konzentrieren.

- Bereite p und a zu Beginn eines jeden Zupfmusters vor.
- Wenn du etwas fortgeschrittener in deiner Zupftechnik bist, bereite jeden Finger vor während der vohergehende gerade zupft.
- Verwende deinen 1. und 2. Finger als Führungsfinger für die ersten beiden Zeilen des Stücks und gleite von Griff zu Griff.
- Verwende Barré-Akkorde von Takt 9 bis 22. Greife dabei nur die Saiten, die du für den Griff brauchst und arbeite daran, jede Position so bequem wie möglich einnehmen zu können.

Practice and Performance Notes

Beneath The Surface is a calm etude that will develop your p-a-m-i picking, your guiding finger technique and your bar chord technique. Imagine looking at an object beneath a water surface, that is slightly changing its appearance while moving upwards, finally breaking the surface.

- Prepare p and a at the beginning of each pattern.
- Once you're more advanced try preparing each picking finger while the previous one is picking.
- Use your 1st and 2nd finger as guiding fingers throughout the first two lines and slide them simultaneously.
- Use bar chords for bars 9- 22. Only fret the strings you need for the chord and make sure every position feels as comfortable as possible.

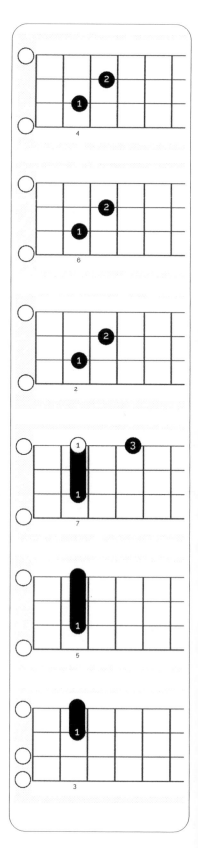

19 Beneath The Surface

guiding fingers / bar chords - Führungsfinger / Barré-Technik / p-a-m-i

19 BENEATH THE SURFACE (TAB)
guiding fingers / bar chords - Führungsfinger / Barré-Technik / p-a-m-i

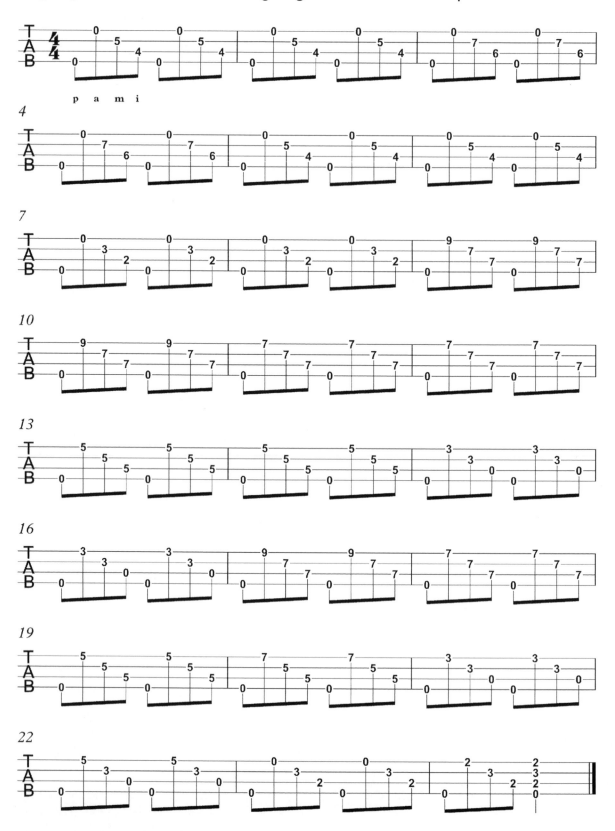

19 BENEATH THE SURFACE (NOTEN)

guiding fingers / bar chords - Führungsfinger / Barré-Technik / p-a-m-i

Tipps und Anmerkungen

Growing ist eine zügigere p-a-m-i Etüde, die sich vor allem mit den Greifhand-Konzepten von Ankerfingern und Führungsfingern beschäftigt.

- In Takt 1- 8 sind dein 1. und 3. Finger Anker- und Führungsfinger.
- In den Takten 1-4 ‚tauschen' dein 2. und 4. Finger.
- Greife die Töne auf der a-Saite in den Takten 13 - 15 mit deinem 4. Finger und verwende entweder deinen 1. oder deinen 2. Finger für die Töne auf der e-Saite.
- Verwende in Takt 16 deinen 2. und 4. und später deinen 2. und 1. Finger.

Practice and Performance Notes

Growing is a faster paced p-a-m-i etude that concentrates on the concepts of anchor and guiding fingers in your fretting hand.

- Throughout bars 1 - 8 your 1st and 3rd fingers are anchor and guiding fingers.
- In bars 1-4 your 2nd and 4th finger 'switch places'.
- Fret the notes on the a-string through bars 13 - 15 with your 4th finger, use your 1st or 2nd finger for the notes on the e-string.
- In bar 16, use your 2nd and 4th finger and then your 2nd and 1st finger.

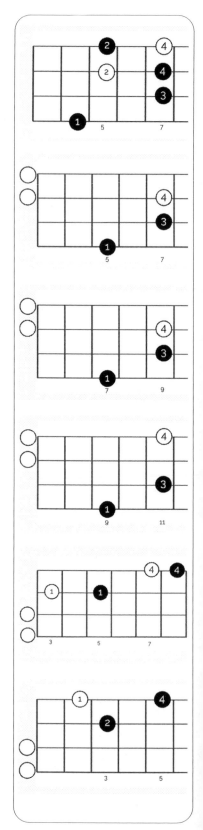

20 GROWING

Anchor fingers / guiding fingers - Ankerfinger / Führungsfinger / p-a-m-i

20 GROWING (TAB)

Anchor fingers / guiding fingers - Ankerfinger / Führungsfinger / p-a-m-i

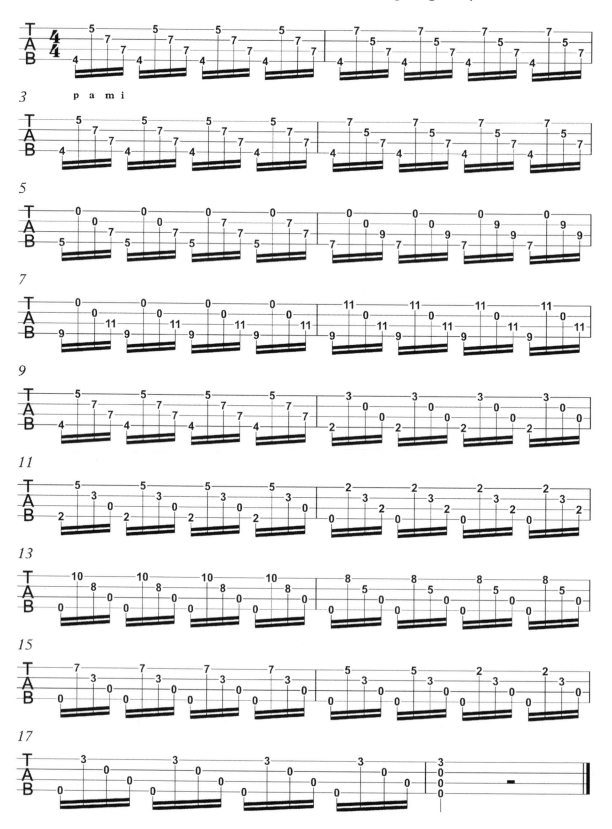

20 GROWING (NOTEN)

Anchor fingers / guiding fingers - Ankerfinger / Führungsfinger / p-a-m-i

Tipps und Anmerkungen

Sing Out ist eine langsame Etüde für das Zupfmuster p-i-m-a, die zusätzlich Anker- und Führungsfinger trainiert.

Adagio heißt langsam, ruhig. Spiele das Stück immer langsamer, als du denkst es spielen zu müssen.

Dein 1., 2. und 4. Finger sind das ganze Stück über Anker- und Führungsfinger

- Dein 2. Finger bleibt immer auf der g-Saite.
- Dein 4. Finger bleibt immer auf der a-Saite, außer in Takt 10.
- In Takt 9 springt dein 1. Finger auf die e-Saite.
- In den Takten 12, sowie 19/20 musst du dich ein wenig strecken, wenn du den 1. und 2. Finger benutzt. Du kannst natürlich auch einen anderen Fingersatz für diese Takte wählen, wenn es anders für dich besser klappt.
- Statt dem 2. Finger, kannst du über das ganze Stück auch den 3. Finger auf der g-Saite benutzen.

Practice and Performance Notes

Sing Out is a slow etude for the picking pattern p-i-m-a, which also heavily concentrates on anchor and guide fingers.

- Adagio means slowly, calmly. Make sure to always play the piece slower than you'd anticipate.
- Your 1st, 2nd and 4th are guide and anchor fingers throughout most of the piece.
- Your 2nd finger always stays on the g-string.
- Your 4th finger always stays on the a-string except for bar 10.
- In bar 9 your 1st finger moves to the e-string.
- Bars 12 and 19/20 are a bit of a stretch using your 1st and 2nd fingers. Of course, you can choose other fretting fingers to make it work for you.
- Instead of using the 2nd finger, you can try using the 3rd throughout the whole piece.

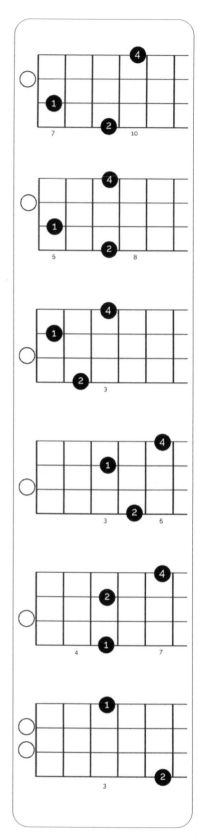

21 SING OUT

anchor and guide fingers - Anker- und Führungsfinger / p-i-m-a

21 SING OUT (TAB)
anchor and guide fingers - Anker- und Führungsfinger / p-i-m-a

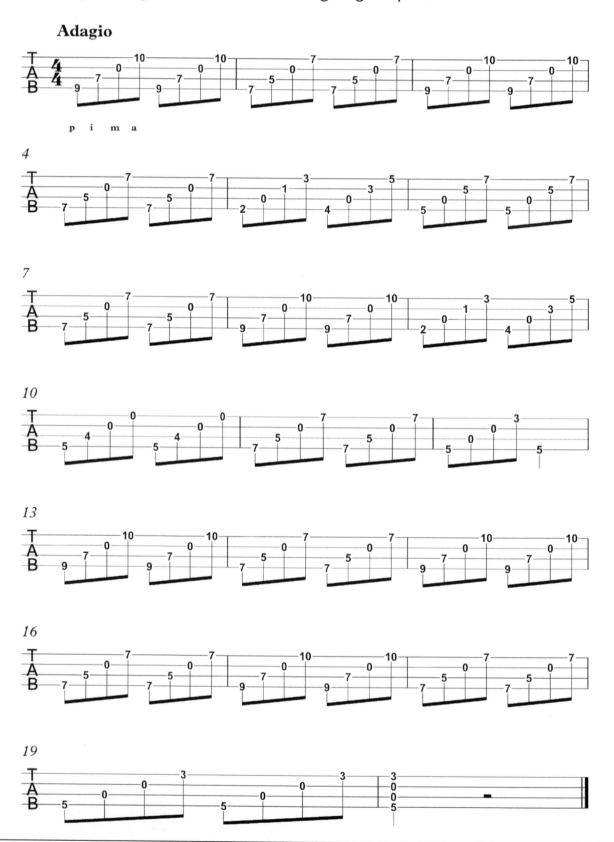

21 Sing Out (Noten)

anchor and guide fingers - Anker- und Führungsfinger / p-i-m-a

Tipps und Anmerkungen

Lily under Water ist eine Arpeggio-Etüde, mit der du das Zupfmuster p-i-m-a üben kannst. Außerdem trainiert sie das Verschieben von Griffen über's Griffbrett.

- Greife alle Töne, die du in einem Takt brauchst (in den Noten und Griffbildern findest du Fingersätze).
- Bewege nur deinen Arm und justiere deine Finger ein bisschen, wenn du Griffe verschiebst.
- Das p-i-m-a Zupfmuster ist hier relativ zügig. Nimm dir Zeit, das Zupfmuster entspannt zu entwickeln.
- Übe das Zupfmuster langsam auf leeren Saiten.
- Bereite immer nur einen Finger vor, d.h. in dem Moment, in dem z.B. p anschlägt, setzt sich i auf die nächste Saite (das nennt man einzeln vorbereiten).
- Erzeuge einen Klangteppich.

Practice and Performance Notes

Lily under Water is an apreggio etude that will develop your p-i-m-a picking and your ability to move chord shapes across the fretboard.

- Fret all the notes you need for one bar in one chord shape (refer to the music and chord diagrams for fingerings).
- When you move chord shapes, make sure to just move your arm and adjust the fingers a little bit.
- The p-i-m-a picking in this is rather speedy. Give yourself time to develop it comfortably.
- Practice the picking pattern slowly on open strings.
- Prepare one finger at a time, i.e. when p is picking, i prepares on the next string (this is a different way of preparation).
- Aim for a sound surface.

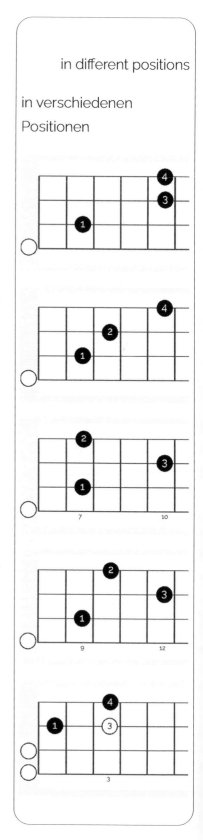

in different positions

in verschiedenen Positionen

22 LILY UNDER WATER

moving chord shapes - Griffe verschieben / p-i-m-a

22 LILY UNDER WATER (TAB)
moving chord shapes - Griffe verschieben / p-i-m-a

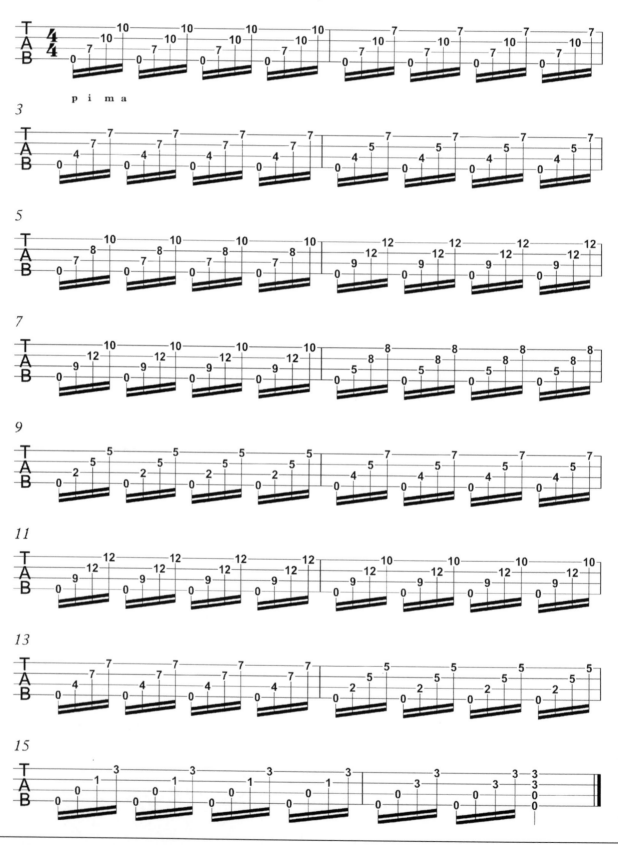

22 LILY UNDER WATER (NOTEN)
moving chord shapes - Griffe verschieben / p-i-m-a

Tipps und Anmerkungen

Alley Way übt dein p-m-a-i Zupfmuster und trainiert deine Fähigkeit einzelne Finger deiner Greifhand zu benutzen, während andere als Ankerfinger verwendet werden.

- Das Zupfmuster p-m-a-i fühlt sich anfangs ungewohnt an. Nimm dir Zeit es langsam auf leeren Saiten zu üben.
- Spiel langsam!
- Suche nach Tönen, die du lange greifen kannst und achte auch auf die Melodietöne, die sich verändern.
- Greife Töne in diesem Stück jeweils so lange, wie es möglich ist.

Practice and Performance Notes

Alley Way will give you a chance to practice your p-m-a-i picking pattern, while training your fretting hand to work with single fingers, while other fingers are anchored.

- The picking pattern p-m-a-i doesn't flow naturally right away. Take your time to practice it on open strings.
- Go slow!
- Look for notes you can fret for a while, but also watch out for changing melody notes.
- Fret notes for as long as possible in this piece.

23 ALLEY WAY
guide fingers - Anker- und Führungsfinger / p-m-a-i

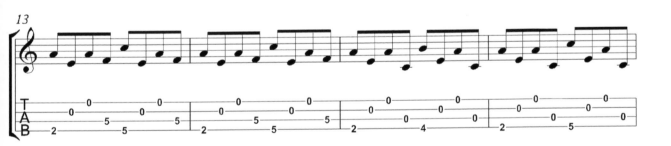

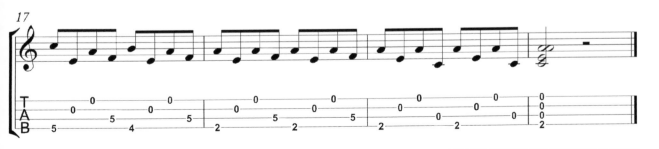

23 ALLEY WAY (TAB)

guide fingers - Anker- und Führungsfinger / p-m-a-i

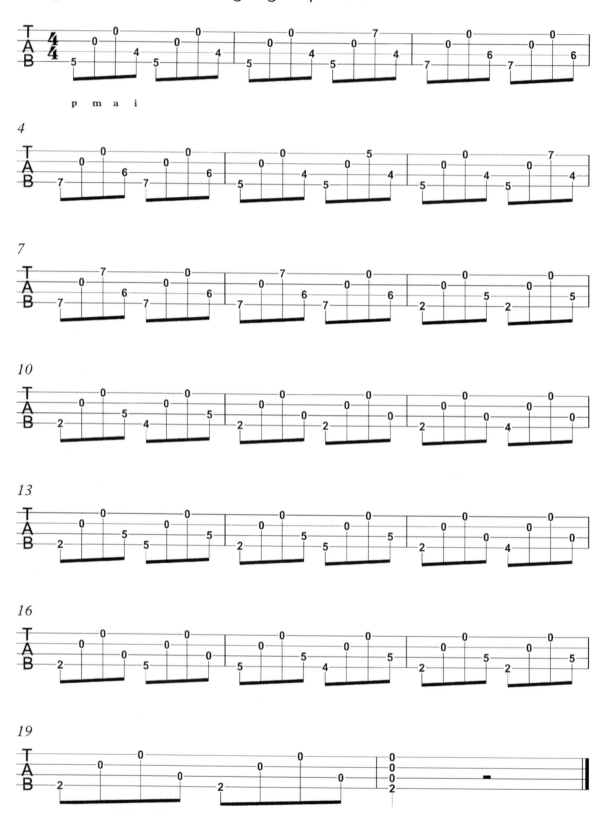

23 ALLEY WAY (NOTEN)
guide fingers - Anker- und Führungsfinger / p-m-a-i

Tipps und Anmerkungen

Helium Balloon beschäftigt sich mit dem Zupfmuster pa-m-i-pa-m-i-pa-m. Bei diesem Zupfmuster wird die rhythmische Betonung der Achtel im 4/4-Takt so verändert, dass zwei 3er-Gruppen und eine 2er-Gruppe aus Achtelnoten entsteht. Dieser Rhythmus kommt in sehr vielen Rocksongs, aber auch südamerikanischen Liedern vor.

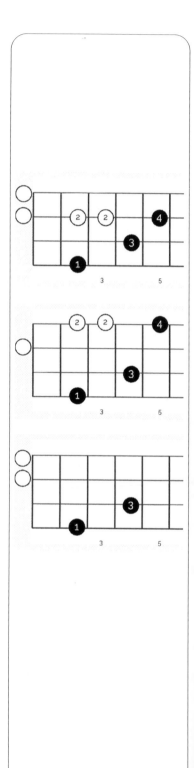

*   Erarbeite zunächst den Rhythmus des Zupfmusters. Die verzwickte Stelle ist der Übergang zum neuen Takt mit der 2er-Gruppe.
*   Sprich ‚Pa-na-ma, Pa-na-ma, Ku-ba' laut mehrmals hintereinander, um ein Gefühl für den Rhythmus zu bekommen.
*   Die Finger 1 und 3 der Greifhand bleiben das ganze Stück über auf ihren Bünden.
*   Mit dem 2. Finger übst du in manchen Takten eine Dehnung. Bleib dabei entspannt!

Practice and Performance Notes

Helium Balloon is about the picking pattern pa-m-i-pa-m-i-pa-m. In this pattern, the rhythmical accents of a 4/4 meter are moved. Now you're dealing with two groups of 3 and one group of 2 eighth notes. This rhythm shows up in a myriad of rock songs, as well as in Latin-American music.

*   Firstly, work on the rhythm of the picking pattern. The tricky spot is the transitional spot to the new bar where you find the group of 2 eighth notes.
*   To develop a feeling for this rhythm, say 'Pa-na-ma, Pa-na-ma, Cu-ba' a few times out loud.
*   Fingers 1 and 3 of your fretting hand stay on their frets the whole time.
*   The 2nd finger goes into a little bit of a stretch in some bars. Stay relaxed!

24 Helium Balloon
anchor fingers - Ankerfinger / pa-m-i-pa-m-i-pa-m

24 HELIUM BALLOON (TAB)

anchor fingers - Ankerfinger / pa-m-i-pa-m-i-pa-m

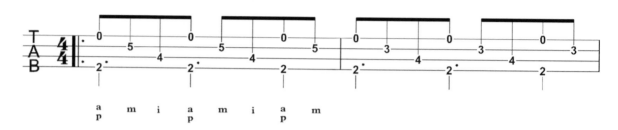

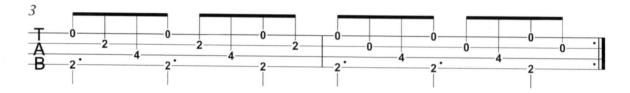

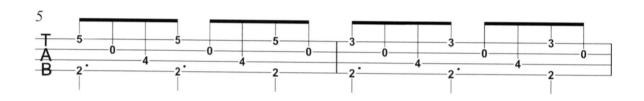

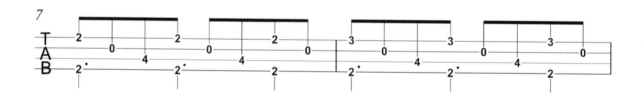

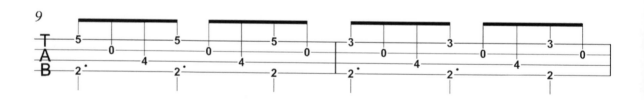

24 Helium Balloon (Noten)
anchor fingers - Ankerfinger / pa-m-i-pa-m-i-pa-m

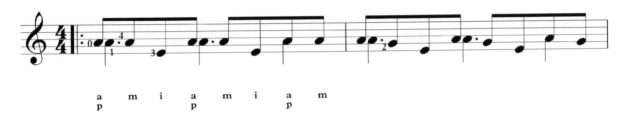

Tipps und Anmerkungen

Running for the HIlls ist eine schnellere pa-m-i-pa-m-i-pa-m Etüde.

- Sprich ,Pa-na-ma, Pa-na-ma, Ku-ba' erst langsam, dann immer schneller.
- Wenn du nicht mehr alle Silben sprechen kannst, reduziere auf ,Pa-- Pa-- Ku--', um ein Gefühl für die rhythmischen Betonungen zu bekommen.

Practice and Performance Notes

Running for the HIlls is a faster paced pa-m-i-pa-m-i-pa-m etude.

- Slowly say 'Pa-na-ma, Pa-na-ma, Cu-ba', then speed it up.
- Once you're too fast to say all the syllables out loud, switch to 'Pa-- Pa-- Cu--', to get a feel for the rhythmic accents.

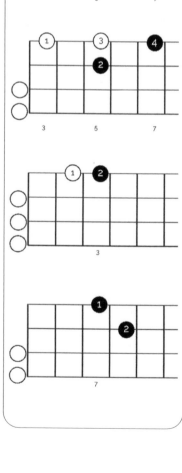

25 RUNNING FOR THE HILLS
guide fingers - Führungsfinger / pa-m-i-pa-m-i-pa-m

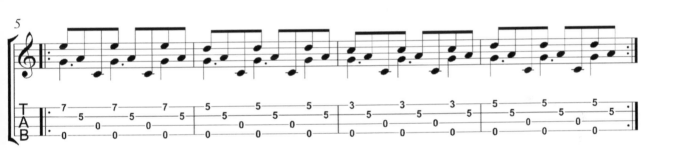

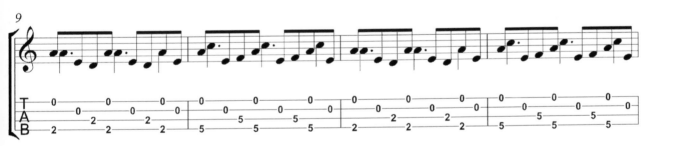

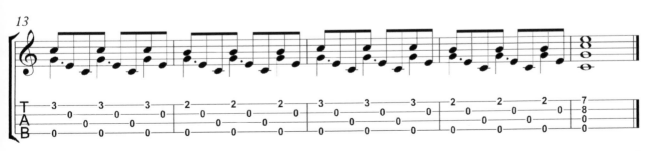

25 RUNNING FOR THE HILLS (TAB)
guide fingers - Führungsfinger / pa-m-i-pa-m-i-pa-m

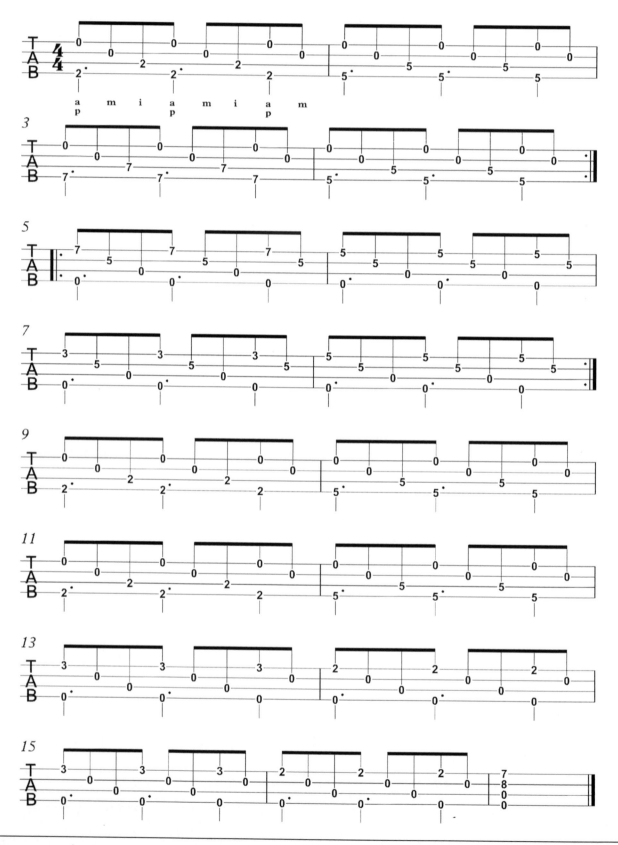

25 RUNNING FOR THE HILLS (NOTEN)
guide fingers - Führungsfinger / pa-m-i-pa-m-i-pa-m

Tipps und Anmerkungen

Sandy Ribbon ist eine Etüde für Einsteiger, die dein p-i-m-i Zupfmuster verbessern wird. Außerdem wirst du dich wohler in höheren
Lagen auf dem Griffbrett fühlen.

- In der ersten Hälfte der Etüde bleibt dein 2. Finger auf der
  c-Saite, außer du spielst die leere c-Saite.
- Verwende den 2. Finger, um in neue Positionen zu gleiten.
- Nimm deinen 3. Finger für Töne auf der e-Saite.
- Im zweiten Teil der Etüde übernimmt der 1. Finger die Rolle des
  2. Fingers und bleibt auf der c-Saite; kombiniere den 1. Finger
  mit dem 2. oder 3. Finger.
- In Takt 13 greifst du mit dem 2. und 3. Finger eine etwas ge-
  streckte Position. Die Dehnung löst sich im nächsten Takt, wenn
  du mit dem 1. Finger am 5. Bund greifst.

Practice and Performance Notes

Sandy Ribbon is an entry level etude that will develop your p-i-m-i
picking and make you more familiar with fretting notes in higher
positions up the fretboard.

- In the first half of the etude your 2nd finger stays on the c-string,
  unless you play the open c-string.
- Take the opportunity to slide your 2nd finger into new positions
- Add your 3rd finger for notes on the e-string.
- In the second half of the etude, your 1st finger stays on the
  c-string; combine it with your 2nd or 3rd finger.
- In bar 13 you start out fretting a stretch with your 2nd and 3rd
  finger. That stretch is resolved in the next bar when you use
  your 1st finger on the 5th fret.

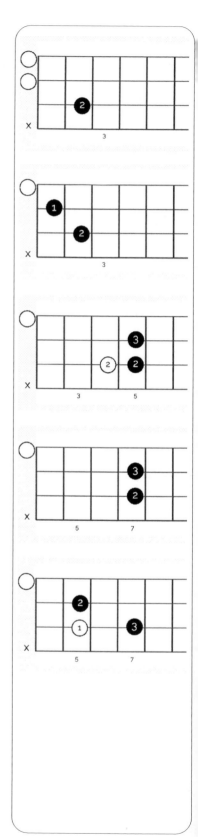

26 SANDY RIBBON
fretting notes in higher positions - höhere Lagen greifen / p-i-m-i

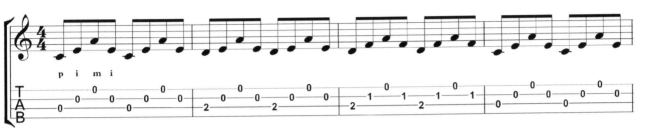

26 SANDY RIBBON (TAB)

fretting notes in higher positions - höhere Lagen greifen / p-i-m-i

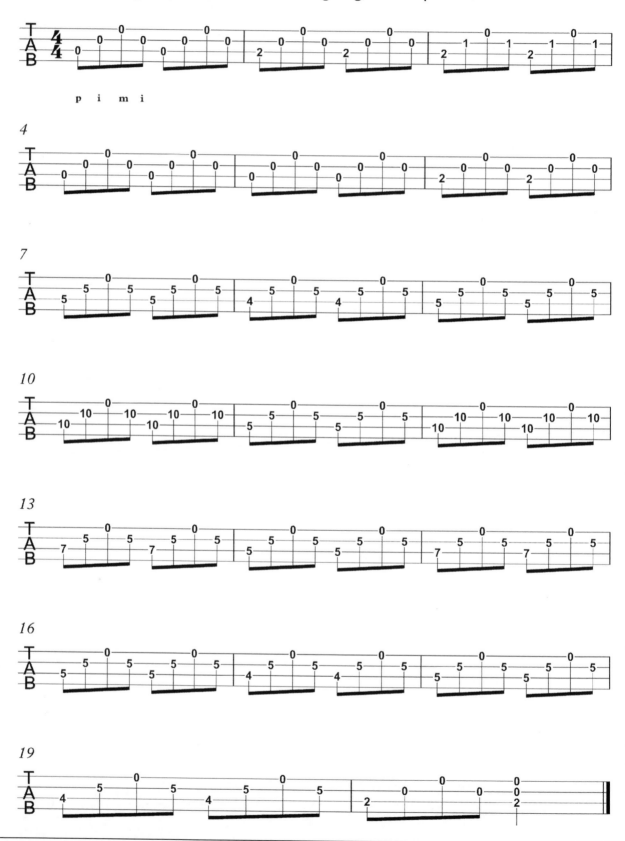

26 SANDY RIBBON (NOTEN)
fretting notes in higher positions - höhere Lagen greifen / p-i-m-i

Tipps und Anmerkungen

Diamond ist eine sehr schnelle (presto) Etüde, die das Zupfmuster p-i-m-i in Verbindung mit ruhigen Griffwechseln trainiert.

- Übe das Zupfmuster unabhängig von den Griffen.
- Halte die Griffe jeweils einen Takt lang.
- Achte auf Ankerfinger.
- Nutze die leere g-Saite zum Griffwechsel.

Practice and Performance Notes

Diamond is a very speedy (presto) etude to develop your p-i-m-i picking pattern while calmly changing fretted notes.

- Practice the picking pattern independently from the fretted notes.
- Hold fretted notes for one bar.
- Look for anchor fingers.
- Take advantage of the open g-string to change fretted notes.

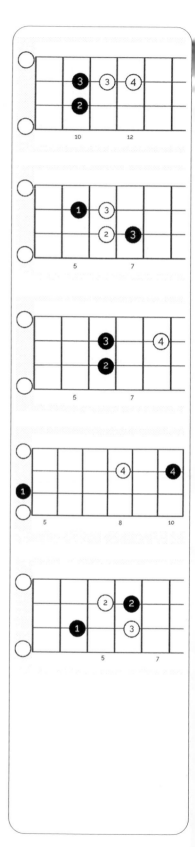

27 DIAMOND
higher positions - höhere Lagen / p-i-m-i

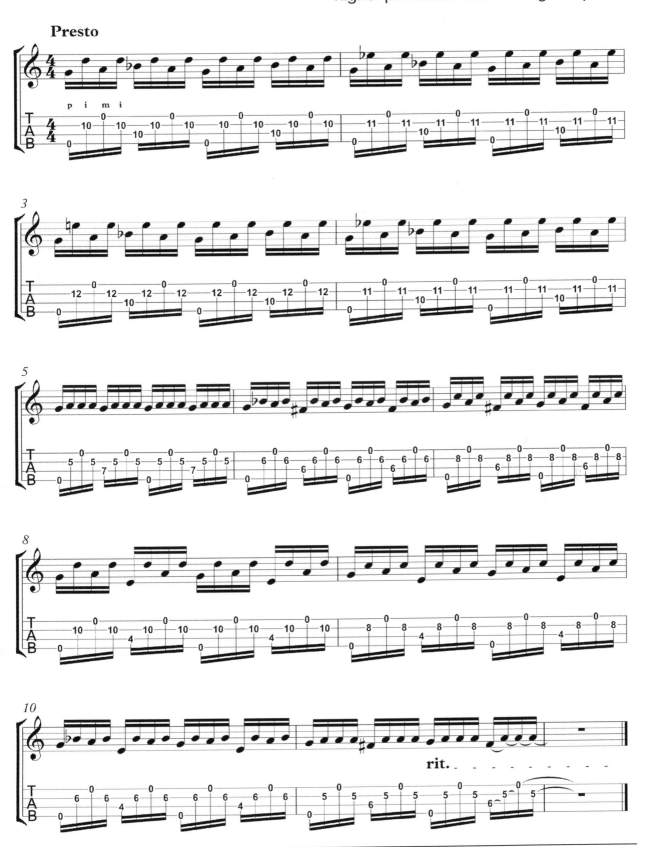

27 Diamond (Tab)

higher positions - höhere Lagen / p-i-m-i

Presto

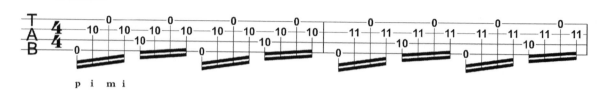

3

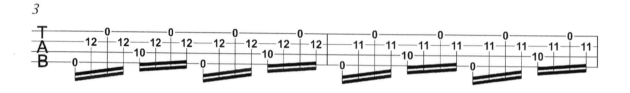

5

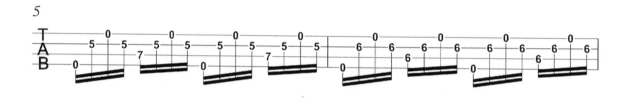

7

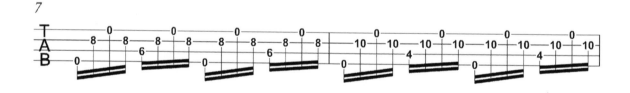

9

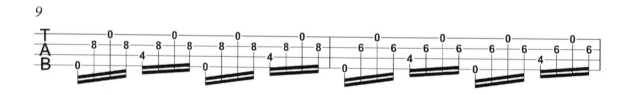

11   rit.

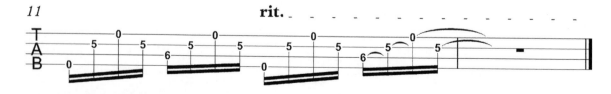

27 DIAMOND (NOTEN)
higher positions - höhere Lagen / p-i-m-i

Presto

p i m i p i m i

rit. _ _ _ _ _ _ _ _ _ _ _ _ _

Tipps und Anmerkungen

Ray ist eine mittelschwere Etüde für dein p-i-m-a-m-i Zupfmuster.

- Bereite i, m und a mit dem Daumenanschlag vor.
- Spiele alle Töne gleichlaut. Zupfe die gegriffenen Töne stärker an.
- Den Griff in Takt 1 greifst du mit dem 1. Finger auf der c-Saite und mit dem 2. Finger auf der e-Saite
- Ab Takt 9 greifst du den gleichen Griff mit dem 2. Finger auf der c-Saite und mit dem 3. Finger auf der e-Saite.
- spiele die leere c-Saite in den Takten 19/20 und 22/23 leiser, damit sie besser zum Gesamtklang passt.

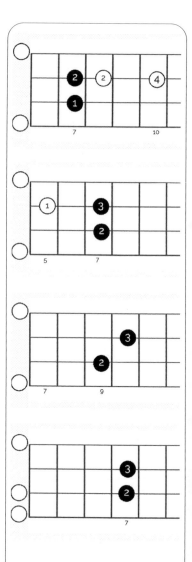

Practice and Performance Notes

Ray is an intermediate etude for your p-i-m-a-m-i picking.

- Prepare i, m and a simultaneously with you thumb picking.
- Play all notes at the same volume. Pick fretted notes harder to achieve this.
- Fret your chord in bar 1 with your 1st finger on the c-string and your 2nd finger on the e-string.
- Fret the same chord in bar 9 with your 2nd finger on the c-string and your 3rd finger on the e-string.
- play the open c-string in bars 19/20 and 22/23 softly make it fit the sound of the rest of the chord.

28 RAY

higher positions / höhere Lagen - p-i-m-a-m-i

28 Ray (Tab)

higher positions / höhere Lagen - p-i-m-a-m-i

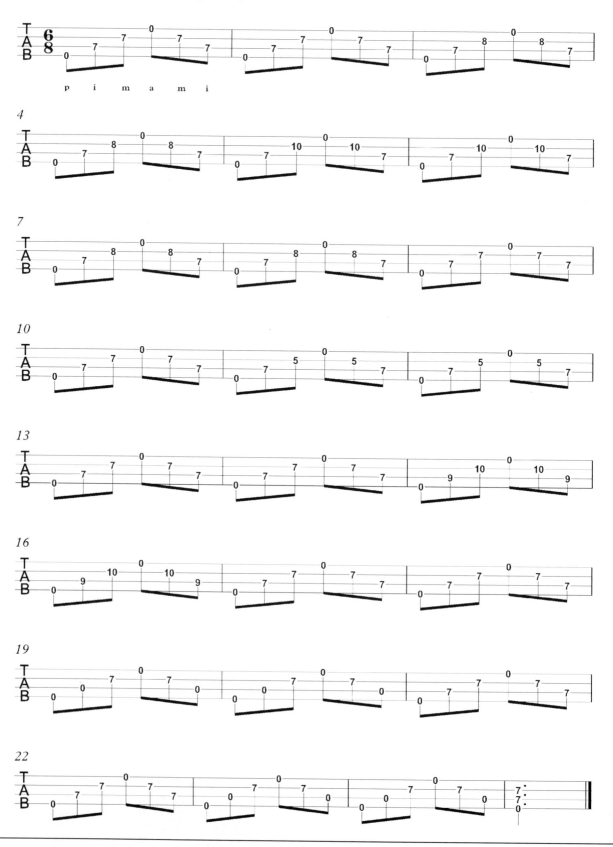

28 RAY (NOTEN)
higher positions / höhere Lagen - p-i-m-a-m-i

Tipps und Anmerkungen

Harlequin ist eine Etüde im mittlerem Tempo, die dein p-i-m-a-m-i Zupfmuster im 6/8-Takt trainiert.

- Starte mit dem 2. Finger auf der g-Saite und dem 4. Finger auf der e-Saite.
- Du kannst jeweils p, i, m und a gleichzeitig vorbereiten.
- Finde eine gemeinsame Daumenposition in der Greifhand für die Griffe von Takt 1 bis 8.
- Im letzten Takt spielst du Flageoletts am 12. Bund: lege dafür z.B. den 3. Finger auf die g- und die c-Saite genau über dem Bundstäbchen des 12. Bundes. Drücke die Saiten nicht auf's Griffbrett und schlage die Saiten stark an, damit du einen glockenähnlichen Flageolett-Klang bekommst.

Practice and Performance Notes

Harlequin is a medium paced etude to train your p-i-m-a-m-i picking pattern in 6/8 meter.

- Start with your 2nd finger on the g-string and your 4th finger on the e-string.
- You can prepare p, i, m and a at the same time.
- Find a common fretting hand thumb position for bars 1 to 8.
- You'll play harmonics in the last bar: place i.e. your 3rd finger flat on the g- and the c-string right above the 12th fretwire. Don't press the strings down onto the fretboard and pick the strings strongly to get a bell-like harmonic sound.

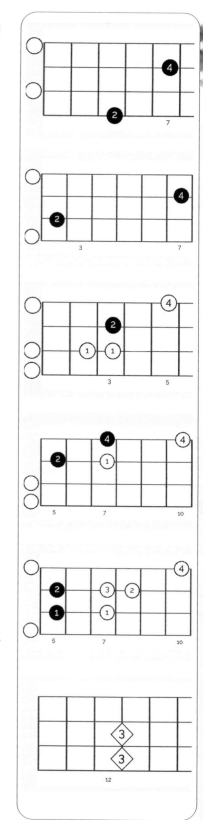

29 Harlequin
guide and achor fingers - Führungs- und Ankerfinger / p-i-m-a-m-i

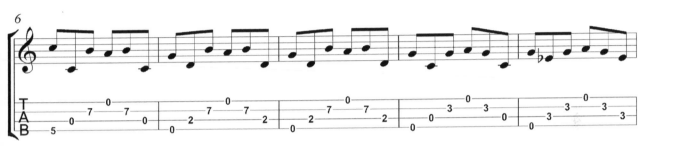

29 HARLEQUIN (TAB)
guide fingers / harmonics - Führungsfinger / Flageolett / p-i-m-a-m-i

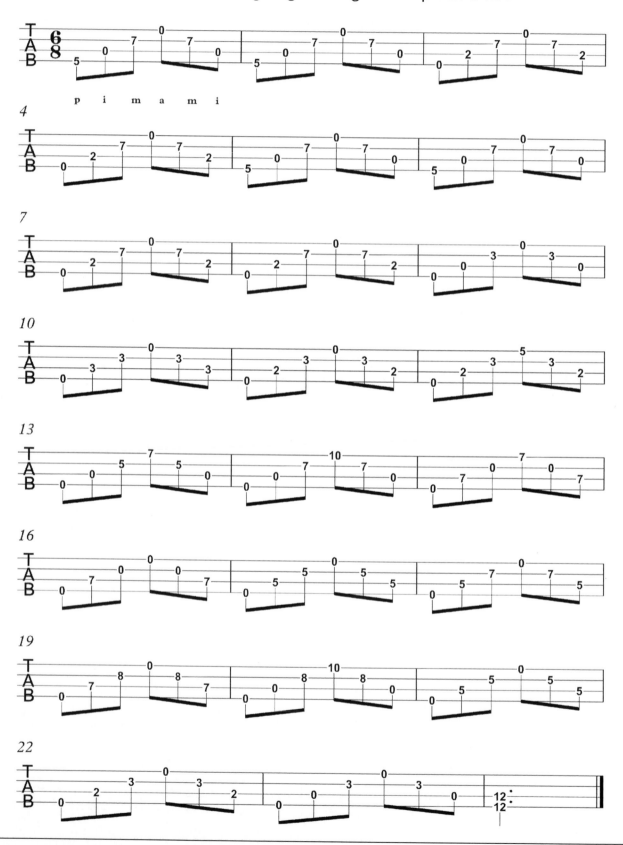

29 HARLEQUIN (NOTEN)

guide fingers / harmonics - Führungsfinger / Flageolett / p-i-m-a-m-i

Tipps und Anmerkungen

Whirl Pool ist eine schnelle Etüde für das Zupfmuster p-i-m-a-m-i.
Dein 4. Finger wird als Ankerfinger benutzt.

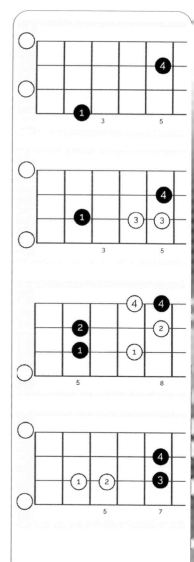

- Übe das Zupfmuster zunächst langsam und spiele nicht zu
  schnell, obwohl das Stück fließen soll.
- Halte deine Zupfhand so ruhig, wie möglich.
- Bereite a, m und i gemeinsam mit dem Daumenanschlag vor.
- Dein 4. Finger ankert auf der e-Saite an verschiedenen Orten
  (meistens am 5. oder 7. Bund), außer in den Takten 9 bis 12.
- Finde gute Daumenpositionen für deine Greifhand.

Practice and Performance Notes

Whirl Pool is a high speed etude for the picking patter p-i-m-a-m-i,
especially concentrating on also training your 4th finger to anchor
in chord changes.

- Practice the picking pattern slow and don't go too fast, even
  though the piece is supposed to flow.
- Keep your picking hand as still as possible.
- Prepare a, m and i the moment you pick your thumb p.
- Anchor your 4th finger on the e-string in different places (mostly
  either 5th or 7th fret) except in the bars 9 to 12.
- Find good thumb positions for your fretting hand.

30 WHIRL POOL

4th as anchor finger - 4. als Ankerfinger / p-i-m-a-m-i

30 WHIRL POOL (TAB)

4th as anchor finger - 4. als Ankerfinger / p-i-m-a-m-i

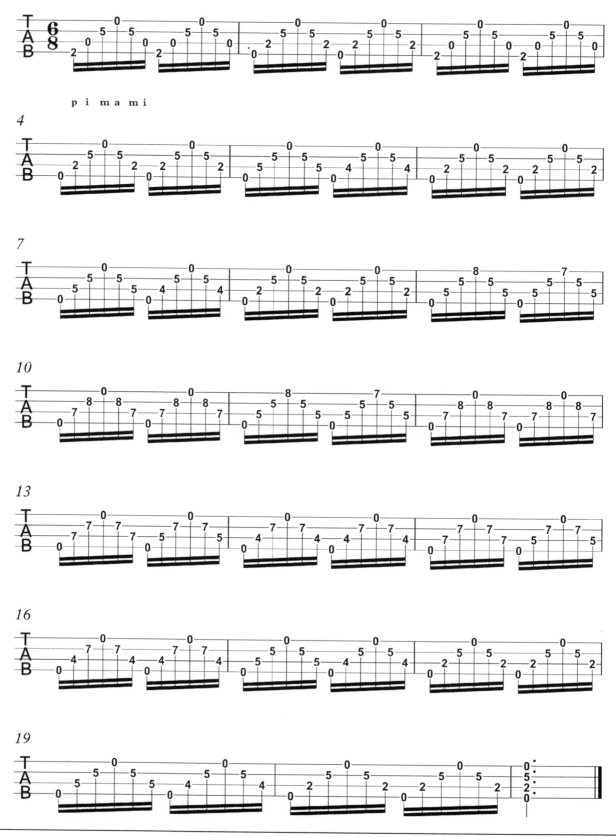

30 WHIRL POOL (NOTEN)
4th as anchor finger - 4. als Ankerfinger / p-i-m-a-m-i

Appendix

AUDIO & VIDEO DOWNLOAD

The audio files and videos are ready for you in a dropbox folder.
Just go to
www.poprockukulele.de/downloads
and
get the link.

Die Audio- und Videodateien liegen in einem Dropbox Ordner für dich bereit.
Gehe einfach zu
www.poprockukulele.de/downloads
und
hol' dir den Link.

The dropbox service is free. Simply register with your e-mail address.

Dropbox ist für dich kostenlos. Registriere dich einfach mit deiner E-Mail-Adresse.

If you have any questions, ideas or problems, please write an email to:

info@poprockukulele.de

Wenn du weitere Fragen und Anregungen hast, oder falls es irgendwo Probleme gibt, melde dich unter:

info@poprockukulele.de

JOIN THE BOOK CLUB!

Make the most of your
Pop & Rock Ukulele Book
in a monthly online Book Club Meeting, that'll showcase one of the etudes in this book:

- general approach
- efficient practicing methods
- exclusive tips and tricks for tricky spots

All meetings will be recorded, so you can watch them later.

KOMM ZUM LESEZIRKEL!

Hol' noch mehr aus deinem
Pop & Rock Ukulele Buch raus und komm zum monatlichen Online-Lesezirkel!
Jeden Monat nehmen wir eine Etüde aus dem Buch genauer unter die Lupe:

- Herangehensweise
- Effektive Übemethoden
- Exklusive Tipps und Tricks zu kniffligen Stellen

Die Treffen werden natürlich aufgezeichnet und können danach noch gekuckt werden.

http://www.patreon.com/elisabethpfeiffermusic

WEITERE BÜCHER   MORE BOOKS

17 Renaissance Stücke von
Adrien Le Roy

17 Renaissance Pieces by
Adrien Le Roy

English:

Deutsch:

Printed in Great Britain
by Amazon

15470402R00084